MOVIE DAD

Finding Myself and My Family, On Screen and Off

Paul Dooley

THEATRE & CINEMA BOOKS

ESSEX, CONNECTICUT

APPLAUSE
THEATRE & CINEMA BOOKS

An imprint of Globe Pequot, the trade division of
The Rowman & Littlefield Publishing Group, Inc.
4501 Forbes Blvd., Ste. 200
Lanham, MD 20706
www.rowman.com

Distributed by NATIONAL BOOK NETWORK

Library of Congress Cataloging-in-Publication Data
Names: Dooley, Paul, 1928- author.
Title: Movie dad : finding myself and my family, on screen and off / Paul
   Dooley.
Description: Essex, Connecticut : Applause, [2023] | Includes
   bibliographical references, filmography, and index. | Summary: "Paul
   Dooley has been an actor for sixty-five years on film, TV, and the stage
   and has appeared in hundreds of movies, shows, and plays. He is best
   known for his roles as the father in Breaking Away, Sixteen Candles, and
   Run Away Bride. Other films include Hairspray, Insomnia, Strange Brew,
   and Wating for Guffman. His TV roles include The Good Doctor, Modern
   Family, Curb Your Enthusiasm, Grey's Anatomy, thirtysomething, My
   So-Called Life, and Star Trek"— Provided by publisher.
Identifiers: LCCN 2022025797 | ISBN 9781493063079 (cloth) | ISBN
   9781493063086 (epub)
Subjects: LCSH: Dooley, Paul, 1928- | Actors—United States—Biography. |
   Fathers in motion pictures. | Fathers on television.
Classification: LCC PN2287.D5243 A3 2023 | DDC 791.4302/8092
   [B]—dc23/eng/20220727
LC record available at https://lccn.loc.gov/2022025797

♾️™ The paper used in this publication meets the minimum requirements of American
National Standard for Information Sciences—Permanence of Paper for Printed Library
Materials, ANSI/NISO Z39.48-1992

Contents

Contents

Contents

Contents

Foreword

It was in the early days of the quarantine. My wife and I were in the kitchen. There was a big pot of vegetable soup over a low flame on the stove. The aroma of it so filled the room I could almost taste it. The sun slanted through the big kitchen window as the dappled light from our neighbors' trees brought the outside inside. Winnie was chopping vegetables and adding them to the soup as we spoke. The way we talked was as much banter as it was conversation. I asked her . . .

"Do you remember my one-man show?"

"I think so . . . who was in it?"

"You're very funny."

"Of course I remember, sweetheart. You were wonderful. Do you want to cut up these peppers for me?"

"The green or the red?"

"Both."

"When was the last time you did any cooking?"

"I don't know . . . when was Nixon elected? I'm putting in some cauliflower."

"I object!"

"You like cauliflower!"

"If it please the court, I do not."

"Overruled. I'm putting them in."

"You know I hate cauliflower."

"So sue me."

"I have nothing further."

"Then I'll see you in Chambers."

"You remember how, for years, people have said to me, 'You've
　　had an interesting life. Why don't you write a book?'"

"Yes, and you always said if it was a book, you couldn't hear the
　　laughs."

"Which is why . . ."

"You wrote the one-man show."

"Exactly. Anyway, I was thinking . . . since we're in lockdown for
　　God knows how long, maybe I'll turn the show into a book.
　　You know, just to keep busy."

"That's a terrific idea! You can even use the same title, *Movie Dad*."

"Exactly."

"And if you need any help just let me know."

"Oh no, no. You have your own writing to do."

"Well, only a ton of it."

"When will the soup be ready?"

"It has to cook for a long time so all the flavors can marinate. The
　　longer it cooks the better it tastes."

"So . . . sometime tomorrow."

"Uh . . . maybe Tuesday."

"I have to admit, honey. I feel a little insecure about this. I've
　　never written a book."

"Well, neither had Dickens 'til he wrote the first one."

"Do you think he got it from his one-man show?"

"Maybe you should just begin by writing the foreword."

"What's a foreword?"

March 2020 (Burbank, CA)

Preface

For the past sixty-five years I've been pretending to be other people. In this book I'll pretend to be . . . myself. Just kidding. I will, I promise, be myself. I am an actor. Well, a character actor. This is the definition of who I am:

char·ac·ter ac·tor

/ˈker(ə)ktər ˈaktər/

noun

An actor who specializes in playing unusual people in supporting, rather than leading, roles.

The character actor is never the star of the movie or the TV show. The audience may find his face familiar but have no idea what his name is. Even though they may have seen him many times, he's still anonymous.

A New York City cab driver once said to me, "I know you." I said, "Oh? Who am I?" He said, "Well, I don't know your name, but you got a household face."

When I was younger, I was never interested in the star of the movie. I liked those characters in the background . . . now I am one.

1
The Founding Father
. . . and Mother

My father's name was PJ Brown. He lived in Parkersburg, West Virginia, a factory town of fifty thousand people next to the Ohio River.

My father's father had abandoned his family. To help out, my dad sold newspapers and delivered laundry his mother had washed for other families.

He left school in the third grade. He had trouble reading anything in a book or on a blackboard because of his poor eyesight. As a result,

My parents in 1920 . . . the happy couple. AUTHOR'S COLLECTION.

he was considered slow. His teacher didn't know he needed glasses. His mother didn't know he needed glasses. And even he had no idea. His was a world just . . . out of focus.

My mother, Ruth, came from a large family, the Barringers, who had seven children. They struggled to make a living, and with seven kids it was not easy. When she was sixteen, her own mother had twins (make that nine kids), leaving her with her hands very full. So, my mother took over the care of the two newborns. She once told me that she was so tired of washing diapers, she married my dad just to "get out of the house." I hope she was kidding.

Obviously they met and married. I don't know the details. I wasn't born yet. They found a home in Parkersburg. My brother, Charles (later called Chuck), was born there.

~

Five years later, my mother was in labor. During a snowstorm, my father left to fetch a doctor. When they got back, I was already there. February 22, 1928.

Me as a baby . . . a part I was born to play. AUTHOR'S COLLECTION.

My father couldn't afford to buy a house, so he saved up and bought two lots outside the city limits for twenty-five dollars each. That's where he would build his own house, and he did just that.

He worked at a factory nearby every day from 7:00 a.m. to 3:00 p.m. and then went to the property and worked on the house until dark. First, he dug a trench and put in a foundation; that took a month. After that he dug a small basement, two months, and put up the framework for one room. That was another month. Often, he used lumber from the scrap pile where he worked. Whenever he ran out of money, he just stopped until he could afford to buy more supplies. Six months went by, now he had three rooms completed and roofed. Once the county put in electricity, he could now work until midnight and sleep there on the floor. Finally, he added an attractive outhouse (there would be no indoor plumbing). In the end the whole thing had taken him more than two years. He did all this by himself and never asked anyone for help. Of course, I didn't see any of this. My mother told me this whole story years later.

The house my dad built, just completed, 1930. AUTHOR'S COLLECTION.

The family moved in when I was two; the house wasn't quite finished, but it was livable.

As a kid I had no idea what my father had accomplished. I thought everyone's dad built his own house.

Years later, in therapy, I realized that my dad, with terrible eyesight, a third-grade education, and never having been an apprentice to any trade, had single-handedly completed all that work. My analyst pointed out that while he may have seemed like an average man with little education, he had to have been very, very intelligent.

My mother had also left school early, just like my father. Between the two of them, they didn't have a lot of book learning, but they both had a lot of common sense. Still, I grew up without a single book in the house . . . well, there was this Bible, but I never saw anyone reading it.

During the Great Depression my father kept his job but had his pay cut in half. Luckily, because of his hard work, we lived rent free.

The house had a living room, which we called the "front room" and was meant for company (who would hardly ever be there). At the opposite end was our kitchen, which featured an "ice box" (there was no refrigerator). Regularly, a man delivered a large block of ice, usually twenty-five pounds. The ice box was insulated to keep it cold, the ice melting very slowly into a metal catch basin until the next delivery.

Between those two rooms was our "middle room." Just off that room was a bedroom for our parents and another I shared with my brother. The middle room, itself, had a couch, a rocking chair, and a sewing machine, and plunked right in the middle of it was a coal stove. One of my chores was to bring in a bucket of coal each evening. The stove would be loaded up before bedtime with enough coal to last the night, except that it never lasted the night . . . by morning the house was cold. My mother was the first one up, and she put more coal in the stove and started breakfast.

Once my father left for work, she would wake me and my brother. Since the house was still cold, she would lay our clothes on the top of the stove's grating for five minutes and then take our warm crispy clothes and put them under the covers so we could sort of get dressed without freezing to death. At the time I took this for granted. Years later I would realize what a thoughtful, caring, sweet thing it was.

My mother was good looking, not beautiful, but handsome. She had a strong face, a sturdy, stocky build, kind of like a pioneer woman.

My dad was shorter than her, kind of bent over, and he seemed to be "old before his time."

~

That rocking chair I mentioned earlier reminds me that my brother and I, and later my sister, were all rocked in that chair and breastfed until we were . . .

Are you sitting down?

. . . five years old.

I learned later that this was not uncommon. But still, I felt some shame, since, after a while, it seemed too much like being a baby. My mother explained that, with little money to spend on milk, many mothers continued breastfeeding as long as the mother's milk was "coming in."

~

I don't have a lot of childhood memories. The earliest one is from when my mother and I were on a streetcar (also called a trolley car), headed for town. We were kind of "dressed up." I had on a little sport coat, a little white shirt, and a little bow tie . . . apparently, I was going to have a little picture taken. A lady on the streetcar noticed me and said:

"Don't you look like the perfect little man? What's your name?"

"Paul Brown."

"Oh . . . are you the coach at Ohio State?"

I didn't know what a coach was, or what Ohio State was. . . . I was five.

"No. I'm just . . . Paul Brown."

Later my mother explained that the man with the same name as mine was the head of a football team at a school. Ohio was across the river from West Virginia, so he was famous even where we lived.

Well, I didn't want him using my name, and I didn't want to use his. This event may be why I was always searching for a new identity . . . and a new name.

~

There were only about twenty families in the area where we lived, and the houses were not close together. On all sides of us, there were empty fields, cornfields, and other gardens. At first, I only played outside in our yard but always inside the fence, and as long as my mother could see me . . . she was okay.

My next boundary was directly across the gravel road from where we lived, where there was a really big field. It looked like a field of wheat but was actually called broom sedge. It stood about three feet high, honey-colored and beautiful. Boys my age, I was six now, would play there every day. Oddly, we played only one game, hide-and-seek. While one of us closed his eyes and counted, the others ran off in all directions, ducked down into the weeds and disappeared. Sounds like fun, doesn't it? No? Well, for us it was. And, as long as my mother could see me . . . she was okay.

When I was seven years old, my territory expanded again. A little ways from our front gate were some low rolling hills that, after school, became my new playground. And as long as my mother could see me . . . she was okay.

Farther up the hills the woods began, with bigger trees that were fun to climb. I was old enough now that even though my mother couldn't see me, she could call me when it was time to come home. And as long as my mother could reach me . . . she was fine.

From then on, I was on my own, trusted enough to leave the neighborhood and come home after a few hours. There was only one rule: Be home in time for dinner, and always before dark.

Only once did I get in trouble. I was headed home but it was already nearly dark. As I came down the road, I saw my father coming my way. He looked angry. We both stopped, staring at each other. He started taking off his belt. My father had never punished me before, so I ducked around him and ran for home. When my dad caught up with me, the belt had been forgotten, and I was never late again. I guess I'd scared them. My mother was angry, and she *really* yelled at me.

And as long as she could *yell at me* . . . she was okay.

My brother was already going wherever and whenever he wanted, paying little attention to Mother. Still, she always warned him each time he went out the door. "Charles . . . I don't care where you're going, just . . . *don't go to the river!*" Chuck would mumble, "Yeah, yeah." As he closed the gate she'd call after him (for the hundredth time), "Remember that Bailey boy drowned there three years ago." "I know, I know," he'd say.

And within twenty minutes he'd be . . . at the river.

The Ohio River was just one mile from our house, and my brother swam there in warm weather, fished there all year-round, and hung out there with his buddies, the . . . "River Rats."

~

The Depression didn't change everything. For my birthday there was always a homemade cake. Still, there was never a party, never any candles . . . and nobody sang "Happy Birthday!" At Christmas I'd get a plaid shirt and a pair of denim overalls, and every three years a winter

7

coat. The first year it was too big and the sleeves were too long, the second year it fit me perfectly, but in the third year the sleeves were too short and the buttons wouldn't close.

On one birthday, I got a BB gun.

My first time as an actor, dressed up as a cowboy.
AUTHOR'S COLLECTION.

But how does a young boy with a BB gun become an actor? Were there signs along the way? Let me think . . . my parents had an insurance policy and once a month, a man would come to the house to collect the payment, which was seventy-two cents. If my mother didn't have the money when he knocked, we would all hide. My brother and I would flatten ourselves against the wall, and my mother would duck behind the couch. The man would peer through the window. When he knocked again, my brother would start to giggle. Our mother would give him a killer look. To her this was serious. To us, it was a game. I loved fooling a grown-up. It was very exciting. For those few minutes, I felt I was "acting." Sure, it wasn't *Death of a Salesman*, except for that salesman.

~

My father was very withdrawn, very remote. Naturally, I wanted to be like my dad. All boys do. So if he didn't smile, I didn't smile. If he didn't laugh . . . same with me. If he didn't show his emotions . . . guess what? Needless to say, I never heard "I love you" from him. I never saw him kiss my mother, or even hug her, and, by the way, he never hugged me. Growing up without a father, I don't think he knew how to be one. Looking back, I think my father tried to do the normal things men did; he married, built a home, fathered children, and worked hard.

You may have noticed I talk more about my father than my mother. It's true. I learned in therapy that the parent who doesn't show you any love, or any affection, that's the one you think about most . . . the one you need but will never get anything from.

When I was four, there was a new baby on the way, so my father built another room onto our house. When she was born, they named her Patricia, but she was always called Patty, and she was a very cute little girl. When she was about two, I would sometimes see her sitting on my dad's lap. He seemed to enjoy having her there. I probably should have been jealous (I would need to speak to my analyst about it someday). I guess my dad thought it was okay to show affection to a daughter . . . but not a son.

~

As a young man I was always wondering *who I was* . . . and *why* I am the way I am. Now I remember something about my mother. As a kid, if I was upset, or on occasion, crying, she had a way of shutting it down as if that was something I should never do.

I wondered, Why?

I couldn't answer that question then, but with two decades of therapy behind me I knew more about it. When a parent hears a little kid crying, the parent may feel a little bit guilty as if he or she had brought on those tears. People don't like feeling guilty. My theory is, if a parent can stop the crying, they'll feel better. Sooo . . . the kid would hear things like, "Don't be a baby," "You're too big to cry," or "I'll give you something to cry about."

Well, if when I cry my mother gets angry at me, the message is I should never, ever cry. That way, maybe she'd still love me. Lesson learned!

~

In the spring my parents would put in a garden. It was very big: four times the size of our house. There were six rows of corn, eight rows of potatoes, one row of lima beans, and another garden with lettuce, tomatoes, cabbage, peppers, and herbs for my mother's cooking. We lived out of our garden. In the summer, a typical meal would be mashed potatoes, tomatoes, lima beans, and corn. We were vegetarians but didn't know the word for it.

In the fall my mother would can vegetables to see us through the winter, and we always had plenty of potatoes in the cellar.

A few years later my father added an outbuilding, actually a garage (although we never had a car). It soon became his workshop. He also built a washhouse (for my mother's washing machine). Next to that was a shed with one side open, and once a year, a man with a dump truck delivered the coal to heat the house. Later still, PJ bought baby chicks, which grew into chickens, so he built a chicken coop, then added a rooster. After that, we always had chickens. He planted grass; there was a lawn and a few trees.

My dad then built a generous front porch, quite wide, with a banister three feet high, and he built a swing as well, which could sit three people. After dinner, my mother would sit there swinging in a slow easy rhythm, often singing, watching friends and neighbors pass by. They'd say hello, gossip for a bit, and be on their way. She enjoyed this socializing; it was sort of like a living newspaper.

After my parents passed away, I had the swing shipped to California. I can see it now in my backyard, with a small brass emblem with my dad's name and the year he built it.

～

My brother, Chuck, was five years older than me. My sister, Patty, was five years younger. Chuck, at fifteen, didn't want to play with a ten-year-old. It was the same with me and Patty. Because of the age difference, we weren't very good playmates . . . except for a few memorable times with Patty.

Whenever there was a summer shower, my sister and I were allowed to go outside (in our underwear) and "run around in the rain." That's right . . . and just that simple activity was so much fun for us; we loved it. We'd run around the backyard and run around the front yard, then all around the whole house . . . stomping in puddles, slipping and falling down in the wet grass, screeching and laughing with the joy of it. I never felt so free.

Chuck was outgoing, confident, and well-liked. Patty and I were both shy, quiet, and well-behaved. We all had chores, and one of mine was gathering eggs. There were twenty chickens, which meant plenty of eggs, more than our family could eat. We gave some of them to our neighbors, and if they had a cow, they'd give us milk.

My sister Patty, me, and my brother Chuck. AUTHOR'S COLLECTION.

~

I walked a mile to school. Probably the worst part of going to school was lunch. There was no money for paper bags, so my mother packed my lunch in yesterday's newspaper and tied it up with string. Of course, string cost money, so she told me, "Don't forget to bring home the string." Every day lunch was the same thing: a sandwich made of Armour Potted Meat Product. What was it, you may ask? It was a . . . tasteless paste, one grade below baloney. My mother would always add a little mayo to make it go further.

The good news was that she always packed a treat: two Graham crackers with chocolate icing in between them prepared the day before. Nobody wanted to trade sandwiches with me (and who could blame them?), but I could always trade my treat for a Moon Pie or a Twinkie. So every day, every day for eleven years, I had a potted meat sandwich for lunch. I didn't like 'em, but I ate 'em. Then, when I became a senior in high school, my mother gave me a quarter every day and said, "From now on you can buy lunch."

What? I thought. *Buy lunch? . . . But where will I find a place that sells potted meat sandwiches?*

Luckily, near the school was a diner where you could buy a "Streamliner," which was a soft, steamed hot dog bun filled with ground beef, sort of like a Sloppy Joe. They were delicious! They were seven cents each. I always got two and had a dime left over for a milk shake.

In my memory, those Streamliners are still the best things I ever ate.

~

But to go back a bit, when I was in the third grade, I fell in love with my teacher. I wrote a poem she liked, and she put it in the school paper. I still have a copy.

Oh, you little Goldenrod
You're such a funny fellow
With your little stem of brown
And little cap of yellow.

You grow along the streamside
Which mostly runs and bubbles
And when the stream is busy,
You never cause it troubles.

You always are so pleasant
And never impolite
And when the summer grass is green
You're such a beautiful sight.

My wife, who actually writes poetry, tells me the poem is about me, that it's a self-portrait. I am the Goldenrod . . . maybe she's right.

In the early grades there would be art classes, possibly to find a budding Picasso, but more likely just to keep the kids busy. None of this helped me. It seems I was "all thumbs" when it came to finger painting.

I had always wanted to draw but didn't know how. So, for my first attempts at home, I would just copy things. I'd put a picture up against a window and then put a blank piece of paper over it and trace the picture, mostly with a pencil, if I had a pencil. By the way, I also never had any crayons, or even a coloring book. Mind you, I'm not complaining . . . that's just the way it was in those days . . . for us artists. When I had nothing to draw with, I would improvise; if it was cold and the window was fogged up, I'd draw on it with my finger.

~

There were some odd nicknames in our neighborhood. The Sink family named one kid "Commodore," a pretty fancy name, but they just called him "Dore." His full name . . . Dore Sink. The Hart family had two kids, "Pig Hart" and her brother, "Frog Hart." Another family had two boys called "Peanuts" and "Popcorn." A neighborhood girl was called Luzetta, a beautiful name. So what did kids call her? . . . Spaghetti.

So many nicknames. I felt left out. I wasn't happy with my name. I was just Paul, and I wanted a nickname too. So I took a pen and wrote "Ace" on my arm; I displayed it whenever I could, but nobody ever called me "Ace." Another time, I drew, on my undershirt, a picture of an airplane and signed it "Skipper." Someone said to me, "What's that Skipper for? Is that the name of the plane?" I said, "Yeah . . . that's the name of the plane." He walked away. Now the plane had a nickname, but I was still . . . Paul.

~

When the Depression ended my dad went back to work on his full salary (still not very much). He usually made $30 a week. On payday he'd give my mother $20 for groceries. There were some things we couldn't get from our garden, like sugar, salt, flour, rice, or mayonnaise. If she wanted to buy anything else, like a housedress for herself, maybe a pair of shoes, cough medicine for the kids, or even needles and thread for her sewing machine, she'd have to squeeze it out of the $20. He didn't have to explain what he spent his $10 on (it was probably something like tools, or work boots; he might even have saved a couple dollars a week). He had one strict rule. Never buy anything on credit!

The summer I was ten, my mother started sending me to the mailbox, about five minutes away. I didn't know why, since my father passed the mailbox on his way home from work. She'd say, "If you find a letter from J.C. Penney, bring it to me. I don't want Dad to see it." I didn't get it, but I found it exciting. It was like a game, like I was a spy. This didn't happen every day, just now and then.

The trouble was, she would sometimes forget this plan until she heard the three o'clock whistle blow, telling her Dad was getting off work and coming right by the mailbox. I would, quick, run down to the mailbox, and sometimes I'd see my father trudging along, always looking down at the road because of his bad eyes, and sometimes very close to me. I'd check for the letter and then duck into a cornfield nearby and run home. I don't think he ever saw me.

My parents didn't argue that often, but when they did, they would just grouse about stuff but never resolved anything. They would just go silent for a few days and then wordlessly drift back to their old ways.

One night, however, I was awakened by a really big fight, yelling and screaming. My dad was furious with my mother, and she was in tears. I heard the name J.C. Penney quite loudly. Apparently, she had opened an account there, forging my father's name to buy some things she wanted. This was a real betrayal for my dad, creating a debt for him he had always avoided. Finally, the yelling stopped. I thought, So, that's what that mailbox business was all about . . . not letting him see the bill from J.C. Penney. He must have paid off the account and canceled it. They didn't speak for a month.

If my mother's "forgery" sounds like a crime—remember, this was the 1930s. A wife could not open an account of any kind, only her husband could do that. Even an unmarried woman with a job would likely need the approval or the signature of her father or another male relative just to open a bank account. So you see, we've come a long way.

⁓

Once, my father indulged himself by buying a radio. Not a little one that would sit on a table, but a big, beautiful console, about four feet tall, in a handsome maple cabinet. Every evening, after dinner, he'd go to the living room, which had two easy chairs and a couch, or what we called a davenport. He would darken the room, turn on the radio, and sit there listening in the glow of the red light of the dial, all by himself.

The family didn't get to listen. We didn't mind. We knew it must have brought him some measure of pleasure at the end of a hard day's work.

This was his radio, his domain. My dad liked mystery programs, but sometimes he'd listen to comedy shows.

~

When I was twelve, I fell in love again. Not with the girl next door . . . no. I fell in love with radio! And all the great radio comedians!

I would edge closer to the wide doorway of the living room and then gradually creep into the room and listen. These comedy programs were filled with wall-to-wall jokes.

> I was born at an early age. My parents couldn't have children, so a neighbor had me.

It didn't matter how dumb they were, I just loved them.

> I was a problem child. At four, I ran away from home, at five, I came back. My parents ran away.

The jokes seemed so personal, like those comedians were there just for me . . . they were my imaginary friends. I soon learned their names. There was Red Skelton, Jimmy Durante, and the great Jack Benny, a man who made millions pretending to be cheap.

> Jack: Gee . . . this is kind of a dark street. Nobody around.
>
> Crook: Hold it right there, this is a stickup! Your money or your life!
>
> Jack: Wait a minute, mister, put down that gun.

Crook: I said, your money or your life!!

Jack: . . . I'm thinking it over.

I also liked George Burns and Gracie Allen

Gracie: My brother lost his job.

George: What happened?

Gracie: Well, he's a window washer, and he was washing a window on the twentieth floor . . . and stepped back to admire his work.

I was intoxicated with all these jokes. The next day I'd re-live them all, finding I'd memorized many of them. I wondered, *What are jokes? What makes them funny?* In my mind I started a never-to-be-forgotten file of funny stuff. Ever since then, if I hear something I think is funny, I never forget it. I'm like an elephant for jokes.

Looking back at myself, at that twelve-year-old kid, hooked on comedy . . . I had to wonder

What kind of an evil demon could cloud the mind of a young boy, take hold of his senses, and enslave him to an uncontrollable obsession . . . with jokes? Oh, I can see how it must have started. Very innocently at first. A pun here, a funny anecdote there. But those are gateway jokes. It could have very quickly led to harder stuff. Mainlining one-liners. Wasted on wordplay. And before you know it, the kid's a wisecrack addict living in a wisecrack house. And where might it all have ended? In the gutter? On Skid Row? Doing "Who's on First" . . . with a homeless guy?

I've got to stop thinking like this.

~

I've been told I have a sense of humor. Well, if I do, I didn't get it from my parents. In fact, my father never said anything funny. And my mother, God bless her, once and only once made me laugh. I told her my teacher asked everyone to put together a family tree. I'd heard Grandma say we had Indian blood.

"Is that true?"
She said, "That's what they tell me."
"Well, how much Indian blood do you have?"
"About a quart."

About a quart? I loved that! My mother was funny! I think I gave her a hug. So, you see, my sense of humor was mostly nature, not nurture. Apparently, I was born this way. It was not a choice.

Now, of course, the proper term for Indian would be Native American, but in the early 1940s that term hadn't been adopted yet.

~

My dad had an "l" fault. He couldn't pronounce any word with an "l" in it. When annoyed he would say, "Hell's bells!" This was a common expression, which came out "Hew's bews!" He called me "Paw," never "Paul." And "Paul Lee" would become "Pawie." He liked to chew tobacco while listening to his radio with me on the rug nearby. He would often keep chewing 'til his mouth started to fill up with tobacco juice. At the last minute, when the juice threatened to spill out, he'd tip his head back and carefully whisper, "Pawie, run out back and git me a spit can."

My job was now to go to a large metal drum out back where we'd throw away our tin cans. I'd rummage around in the dark, hoping to find one without a sharp lid on it, and run back in with it. Disaster averted! This would happen about once a week.

Finally, to avoid this Niagara of overflowing juice, I'd find a can during the day, hide it on the back porch, and always have it at the ready. He also had a "th" fault. My mother's name, Ruth, became "Roof," and when he was mad at her she was just "Woman." As in, "Goddammit Woman! Where's my dinner?" (His dinner was always on time.)

2
Gold Nuggets

My grandparents lived near us, just ten minutes away. My mother would often take me and my sister for a visit. Chuck was always off with friends. My dad never, ever, went there. There were usually a lot of people around since some of my aunts and uncles lived nearby as well.

One night, there was a new person there. Everyone seemed to know him. He had grown up around this family and knew my mother from school; they seemed to have a connection. He traveled around a lot and did construction work, but he was now back in town. They called him Gil.

This fellow was a charmer. He told stories, played guitar, and was the center of attention. He had just come back from Colorado and was showing around nuggets with streaks of gold in them. He gave one to me. We would see him there off and on.

One night we were heading for Grandma's house when we saw on the dark road ahead a car sitting there with its lights dimmed. It was almost scary. My mother said, "I have a surprise for you." She was putting something red on her lips. . . . I had never seen her do this. "We're not going to Grandma's tonight," she said. "We're going to the movies. Don't say anything to Dad. You know how he is; he doesn't want anyone to have any fun." Wow! I thought. This is gonna be great! Before this I had seen very few movies.

I can't remember the film, but my guess is it wasn't for kids. I liked watching it anyway. Patty and I sat down front, and my mother and Gil were a row behind us. The next time we went they sat farther back. We did this every couple of weeks, and once, when I looked back, they weren't even watching the movie.

A few times, my mother gave us our tickets and told us they wouldn't be going in, but they'd be parked outside waiting for us. I thought, *Okay. As long as I get to see the movie.* After a while it all stopped. No more movies, no more Gil. My mother said he had left town. I was disappointed. I had kinda liked him. After all, he gave me a gold nugget every time I saw him.

In my thirties, I was in therapy and dimly remembered those times. My analyst helped me understand it all. My mother was having an affair. I could hardly blame her. Hers was a loveless marriage, and she was in need of some affection . . . however brief.

Now that I'm older and wiser, I see all that from another perspective. It's true, I guess, my mother chose to cheat on my father. The question is, why did she involve me, making me a part of her betrayal?

My father deserved better.

3
Forty Feet Up

A little ways from our back gate, there was a bridge over a small creek called "Pond Run," which was never more than two feet deep. I had practiced "mud crawling" there, kicking my feet and crawling on the mud bottom until I learned to "dog paddle."

Beyond the bridge there was a glass factory, a marble factory, and a silk mill, and then you would find Route 21, a major highway that ran for miles near the Ohio River. We didn't really live in a town, we lived in a no-man's-land between two towns.

Nearby was the Stonewall Inn. It was just a place to buy candy, soda pop, potato chips, and take-out beer. (West Virginia was a dry state, so you couldn't sell "hard liquor.")

Down a sloping bank, behind the Stonewall, you would take an overgrown path through a tall cornfield. Then the bank plunged diagonally down toward the water, and there it was . . . the Mighty Ohio.

There was an old tree there, fallen years ago into the river and dragged by the current downstream and lodged next to the bank. A fork in the tree created a Y, and over time, a makeshift platform had been built there to dive from. This is where the younger boys spent their time. We called it "The Log."

Just a few yards upstream was a giant oak tree, a century old and as tall as a building six stories high and so big it would take three men's arms to encircle it.

The tree, constantly reaching for the sun, leaned out over the river at an extreme angle. There were no lower branches, and it seemed impossible to climb, yet my brother, Chuck, had done just that.

He had climbed up that tree trunk like some kind of monkey carrying a small rope. Once up there, the rope was attached to a sturdy cable and hauled up. My brother had then wrapped the cable twice around a large branch, had taken a metal U-bolt from his pocket along with some nuts, and, using a wrench, tightened it all up and come down. No one else could have done it. Not only was it kind of dangerous, but it took a lot of know-how, and I wondered, *Could my brother understand building like my father did?*

Back on the ground, Chuck pushed the bottom end of the cable through a metal pipe, lifted it up to join the longer cable, and attached it also with a U-bolt, creating a "trapeze-type bar."

When it was all in place, ready to go, you could climb partway up the bank, swing out, and drop off at twenty feet into the river. All the way to the top of that steep bank gave you a forty-foot drop-off. It was spectacular! . . . but not for the likes of me.

The swing belonged to my brother and his friends; no younger kids allowed. We could only watch. At about three o'clock, the older boys left for their afternoon shifts at summer jobs, leaving the swing to us.

All us kids swam naked and did our swinging naked. There were never any girls there. Well, hardly ever. From time to time, someone would yell, "There's a girl here!" We would all scramble for our pants, but it was usually too late. She would be standing at the top of the bank, a cigarette in her hand.

Lillian was fourteen and a tomboy. All of us guys would retreat to the river. Lillian enjoyed toying with us, trapping us in the water. We would stand there up to our waists as she sat there smoking one cigarette after the other for twenty minutes. Then, with a wicked smile, she was gone.

I loved practicing on the swing. I would swing out all the way, and at the end there would be a moment, really just a second, when I would be weightless. Then I would let go and do what we called a "needle drop." On the way down, I would pull my knees up, as if sitting in a chair

Me on the spectacular swing, my brother climbing the tree. AUTHOR'S COLLECTION.

pretending to read and smoking a pipe. I can see now that this was just the . . . (as yet unknown) actor in me trying to get attention.

During that first summer, I worked on perfecting my aerial skills. When the swing reached the end of its arc, I would be nearly horizontal. I would let go and easily do a back-swan dive.

Summer after summer I improved until I was able to perform a backflip, a one-and-a-half flip, and finally, a two-and-a-half flip from forty feet up.

I only wish I could share with you the excitement, the sense of freedom I felt flying out over the water, the wind in my face; and just imagine how thrilling it was . . . when I was naked.

Okay, that's enough imagining.

4
Living on the River Bank

When World War II started, Chuck, just shy of seventeen, told Dad he wanted to quit school and join the Navy on his next birthday, but he would need Dad to sign his papers. "You're not joining anything!" Dad told him. "If you quit school, you have to go to work. I'll get you a job at the plant."

My brother spoke up, replying, "No! I'm not going to waste my life at that goddamn factory the way you have!" Chuck had never "talked back" like that to him. My dad was insulted. He got angry and they both started yelling. My father, who'd never punished any of us before, took off his belt and threatened to give my brother a whipping. Chuck yanked the belt away from him, pushed him down into a chair, and stormed out of the house.

My dad was angry at having his authority challenged for the first time. For days my brother stayed away. My mother had a feeling she knew where he was.

A year before, Chuck and his friends had built a shanty on the river-bank constructed of scrap lumber and driftwood. One wall was a large Coca-Cola sign made of tin, and there was even a rusty Stop sign on the door. I was sent to find him and tell him to come back home. Dad was too stubborn to go look for him, and Chuck was too stubborn to come back. This went on for months.

Chuck was very resourceful. He had built himself a rowboat earlier, and now he fished every day, taking his catch door to door and selling it for twenty-five or fifty cents. What he didn't sell he'd have for himself. He also began to trap muskrats, setting traps along the river's edge. He would then skin them, gut them, hang them on a line to dry out, and sell them to J.C. Penney for a dollar a pelt. The company would then use them for trim on winter coats, calling them, I'm sure, rabbit . . . not muskrat.

When he turned seventeen, Chuck came back home hoping he'd get his papers signed. Dad, who was now sick of it all, signed, and Chuck finally joined the Navy.

~

In the eighth grade, I chose a class in Home Ec, because I knew it would be mostly girls. It seemed like a good way to get a girlfriend. Instead, I fell in love with the teacher. Her name was Miss Meadows, and she was a knockout, about twenty-five, very beautiful and very curvy. I think, because I was the only boy, she paid more attention to me. I convinced myself that she was in love with *me* too.

After summer vacation I found I couldn't take another Home Ec course, and I also learned that Miss Meadows was now . . . Mrs. Nelson. She had gotten married! I was heartbroken! *How could she?* I thought. *How could she?* It took a long time for me to get over her. I didn't learn much about love . . . but I did learn how to make a muffin.

~

Finally, I was in high school, and I saw, for the first time, in a variety show, a student who could juggle. He was good. He could keep three or four balls in the air. I liked that a lot and decided to teach myself to do it. I didn't have balls of any kind, but I lived on a gravel road and found three rocks to practice with. And, after dropping them about a thousand times, I finally mastered three-ball juggling. For a moment I thought, *Okay . . . I could be in show business!*

On December 7, 1941, the Japanese attacked our country at Pearl Harbor. The president declared war on Japan, and later, on Germany as well. I began drawing planes, tanks, and pictures of Hitler.

5
The Great Stone Face

When I was fifteen, I took an art class. One day, I was probably drawing a bowl of fruit, when I glanced over at my neighbor, who seemed to be drawing an actual cartoon. I couldn't believe that someone sitting next to me was doing that. His technique was very professional. I was impressed.

At that moment I thought, I want to do that! I felt I never wanted to draw anything realistic ever again. No more planes, or tanks, and goodbye Hitler! I was going to be a cartoonist.

That artist was Jim Dukas, and his cartoons were for the school paper. We became friends, and I started to do cartoon characters too. At first I copied Jim, but he encouraged me to be more original, and although I didn't know the word for it yet . . . I had a mentor.

One day Jim invited me to his house after school, telling me he had something to show me. It turned out to be his collection of silent films. Jim had his own 8mm projector and screen (his family was well-off; mine was not). He threaded the film, dimmed the lights, and turned on the projector, and there, flickering before me, was the image of a man acting out a story, and doing it hilariously . . . without words. Jim said, "That's Buster Keaton." He was a comic, an acrobat, and a wonderful actor. No matter what was happening to him, he never smiled. That moment had a profound effect on me. It was as if Jim Dukas was Thomas Edison, and I was . . . well, me, discovering film for the first time.

He also showed me movies with the great Charlie Chaplin, whom I learned was considered the genius of silent films. He was incredibly talented, but for some reason I kept thinking about Buster Keaton. Chaplin I could admire from afar, but somehow, Keaton seemed more real, more accessible. I felt I knew him; or wanted to.

In the 1920s these great comedians were world famous. With no language barrier, they were enjoyed not only in America but in Africa, China, Japan, and all over Europe. Each of these comics had created his own character. Chaplin was called "The Tramp." Keaton was "The Great Stone Face." There were also the Keystone Cops, a ragtag band of idiots who

Silent film comedian Buster Keaton, who became my hero. AUTHOR'S COLLECTION.

chased the comics across the landscape, never catching any of them. The moment I saw Buster Keaton, I knew, somehow, I wanted to do what he did. Of course, nobody could do what he did, but I wanted to try . . . to become a comic actor.

Jim and I went out on weekends to make silent films of our own using his 8mm camera. At secondhand stores, we found derbies and top hats and canes (oh my!). We even bought day-old pies, not to eat, just to throw! We were not very funny, but our short films really had the look and feel of those early silent films.

Jim was just a year older than me but at age sixteen, he seemed even older. He was already a character actor, playing parts onstage of men forty or fifty years old. Jim was Greek, and he had an ethnic look about him, a craggy face, and could easily play the heavy because he was . . . heavy. He also had a very deep voice, dramatic, resonant. He had become the one student who competed in public speaking contests around the state and always came home with first prize. Jim wasn't originally from West Virginia; he had lived in Cleveland for a time. All the rest of us had West Virginia accents, kind of a twang, but Jim spoke

That's me in my own silent comedy *Trouble at the Beach*. AUTHOR'S COLLECTION.

a perfect Standard American Speech.

During the war, one by one, the announcers at our local radio station were drafted into the Army. The station was having a hard time replacing them when they heard about this high school student with this great voice and promptly hired him. At age sixteen, Jim became a real radio announcer, partly because of that voice, but also because he brought with him his huge record collection of Big Band music and jazz. Here he was making a good living from four to ten o'clock in the evenings, doing news, weather, and music, while still in high school.

At Jim's suggestion I took a theater course and was cast in my first play, Shakespeare's *As You Like It*. This would be a great story if I said that's when I found I loved acting, but that didn't happen. Because I wasn't doing comedy, I found it kind of boring.

~

I was assigned to a new homeroom. One of my classmates, Bob Lichello, started a one-page newspaper called *The 315 News*. He made copies for everyone on a mimeograph machine. He had a wild sense of humor and would report news items about students and teachers, all made up. He named a school nurse Miss Coronary Thrombosis. In another time, he would likely work for *Mad* magazine. He knew I liked jokes and asked me to do a humor column in his little newspaper. I borrowed my jokes from the radio. The two of us had a lot of fun and were to stay friends in college.

~

A couple of years later it looked like the war in Europe might be winding down; the US Army had taken Italy. My brother's ship was anchored offshore, and he paid a visit to Rome. The next time he came home he brought me a souvenir. It was a small object about two inches long made of silver. It was definitely a penis with testicles and, strangely, a pair of wings attached. I asked him, "What is this?"

"It's a Flying Cock and Balls," he said. I was confused. He went on. "See, years ago most people couldn't read. Shopkeepers didn't have signs on their stores. Instead, they hung out something else. The tailor had a huge pair of scissors outside. The shoemaker had a big shoe out front." So I asked him, "What is *this* for?" He said, "Well, there's a giant one of these outside . . . the bordello." I said, "What's a bordello?" I was fifteen. "It's a whorehouse," he confided, "where men would go to have sex with women." "What about the wings?" I asked. He laughed and said, "I guess they mean . . . come in here and your cock and balls will fly away to heaven."

I said, "Oh, okay . . . thanks." I kept it hidden in my room for a while, then threw it away, afraid my mother would find it.

~

In time, my friends and I were just a gang of four: Harold, Ab, Junie, and me. We were all in our teens, and when Junie got his driver's license, his dad loaned him his old Hudson every Saturday night.

So we'd go out looking for fun . . . which meant looking for girls. I swear to God, we drove around for the better part of a year and never, I repeat never, picked up any girls. What we seemed to forget was that, even if we picked up four girls, they'd never all fit in the Hudson, plus, why would four girls find *these* four guys attractive. We were so stupid.

But stupid or not we still had fun. The kind of fun teenage boys had . . . *not* finding girls. That 1938 Hudson had a radio, and we could listen to Big Band music with bandleaders Benny Goodman, Artie Shaw, and Harry James and singers Bing Crosby, Rosemary Clooney, and Frank Sinatra. We sang along (off-key) to the popular songs of the day: "I'll Be Seeing You," "We'll Meet Again." "P.S. I Love You," and of course, "Don't Sit Under the Apple Tree with Anyone Else but Me," by the Andrews Sisters. Many of these songs appealed to young women pining for a soldier far away.

Our friend Ab (short for Albert) played guitar, so sometimes we'd turn off the radio and listen to him play. Ab's parents were churchgoers, and all he knew were hymns . . . so we sang along to "Yes, Jesus Loves Me" and all the other churchy songs on the Hit Parade.

When I was sixteen, my mother would give me a dollar every Saturday night to spend on myself. I couldn't believe it! A whole dollar! Late on Saturday nights we'd end up at White Castle for a dozen tiny burgers, some french fries, and Cokes. By the way, none of us drank or smoked . . . or even got laid, so how much fun were we really having?

Here's the weird part. During all that time, we never once went to a movie. It just never occurred to us. There were movies around; I don't know why I didn't suggest it. Here I was wanting to maybe be an actor and still not finding a way to watch the movie stars of that time. For just twenty-five cents, I could have seen Jimmy Stewart, Henry Fonda, even Spencer Tracy.

What a missed opportunity.

Maybe I was just thinking that none of them could be as good as Buster Keaton.

6
Funny Faces

My friend Jim graduated, and I inherited his job on the school paper. I was now the staff cartoonist, and seeing my work in print was exciting. I entered a cartoon contest in *Scholastic* magazine and won a prize. A twenty-five-dollar war bond.

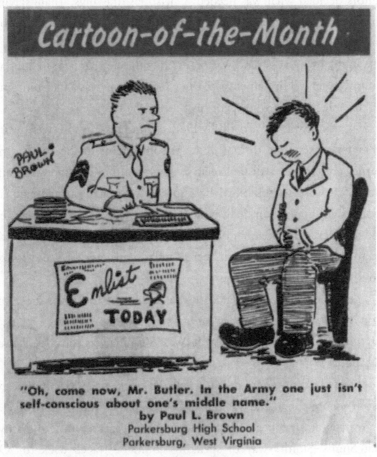

The prize-winning cartoon. BY PAUL DOOLEY

I started to wonder . . . *cartoonist? Maybe that's the definition of who I am now?*

car·toon·ist
/kär ' toonəst/
noun
An artist who makes humorous drawings or cartoons.

My cartoons for the school paper were not always my choice. The editors decided what was needed. Christmas drawings, Thanksgiving, and Halloween were popular, and cartoons about our school's football and basketball teams were also featured.

On my own, however, I was obsessed with one character in Sunday's "funny papers." His name was Barney Google. He was a half-pint, raffish, lovable gambler who spent his time at the racetrack.

His creator was the artist Billy DeBeck, and his cartoons were *exactly* what I wanted mine to look like. At some point in the comic strip, Barney goes to visit a distant relative down South; his name was Snuffy Smith. He was a real hillbilly whose speech was practically a foreign language. I got hooked on the way he talked. The word "ate" became "et," and to describe the weather once, Snuffy said, "Looks like it's clabberin' up to rain." I knew that "clabbered milk" had gone bad and looked cloudy; it kind of made sense.

Snuffy became so popular with the readers, he took over the comic strip, now called *Barney Google and Snuffy Smith*. Why was I so interested in this hillbilly culture? Well, West Virginia was considered a sort of hillbilly state.

I created my own comic strip. I called it "Zeke and Zeb." It appeared in our school paper, and I shamelessly copied the Snuffy Smith style.

Years later, in college, I was studying Shakespeare, only to discover that Snuffy Smith's way of speaking could be traced back to "Old

English." I found that the past tense of "eaten" was "et," and "heated" was "het" (as in "all het up"), and so on.

It seems that some folks who came to this country were Scotch and English, and some settled into the hills down South in small villages isolated from the mainstream. Over the years, their speech didn't change much.

~

Finally . . . the war was over! They declared VE Day! Victory in Europe!! People were in the streets (well, in the fields), cheering and embracing one another. The tensions of the war had evaporated. We were still fighting the Japanese, but shortly afterwards, they surrendered as well. Now it was peacetime, and everything could go back to normal.

With the war over we knew my brother would be home soon. One of my cousins told me he had seen Chuck at a movie theater in a newsreel. I went to see it. There was a short film clip with my brother coming down the gangplank of his ship holding a puppy. The announcer explained there had been a pet on the ship and Chuck had ended up with it.

When Chuck arrived, the little dog was in a kind of makeshift wheelchair; its hind legs were paralyzed. He explained that a German submarine had been sunk by his ship and some of the German crew were swimming around in the water with the little dog floundering by himself. The German sailors were taken aboard and held as prisoners; the dog became a mascot. My brother was a gunner, and he used an empty shell casing to make a roller and a frame for it so the little dog could roll himself around. In fact, my brother had named him Rollaround.

My mother didn't like that name. She decided he was hers now and called him "Poo-gee." He was around for just a year, but he was full of life and rolled around happily in his little cart until the end, little knowing he was handicapped.

I graduated from high school in June of 1945. I was not an outstanding student, nor even really popular. I never dated. I didn't go to the prom. And for the yearbook photo, I had to borrow a sport coat, a shirt, and a tie from my cousin.

Not sure what I might be doing next, I took a job at Universal Glass, a factory ten minutes from my house where they manufactured milk bottles.

~

Even though the war was over, the draft was still going on. This didn't make sense to me. After all, if there was no more fighting, why would the Army still need soldiers?

Then I learned the reason. The Army needed to immediately bring home all those men who had done the fighting and replace them with fresh recruits to maintain the military camps all over the world. I had been given a draft number and was just waiting to be called up on my next birthday. It would be only a matter of time before I'd be a soldier.

So, to avoid the Army . . . I joined the Navy.

I'm sure I picked the Navy because that was my brother's choice. I was sent to the Great Lakes Naval Training Center, where there would be no time to listen to radio comedy or watch Buster Keaton films. I would be totally immersed in basic training.

On day one, I found myself standing in a big room with about forty other men . . . all buck naked. You

In the Navy; *not* the most fun I ever had. AUTHOR'S COLLECTION.

know how they say: "All men are created equal." Well, from what I could see . . . that was not exactly true.

We were lined up and hurried through physical exams. We were given our uniforms, our boots, our backpacks, and a kit of toiletries: washcloth, soap, razor, and so on. I asked the guy next to me, "What's this?" "It's your toothbrush." I must have looked confused. "For brushing your teeth, dummy!"

"Oh . . . I knew that."

Are you sitting down? . . . I had never seen a toothbrush.

"How is that possible?" you might ask. At that moment I had no idea. I was embarrassed; I felt like a real hillbilly. Since then, I've figured it out.

Both my parents were born around 1900. At that time, dentistry was very primitive, especially in small towns. Dentists only pulled teeth; there were no cavities filled, no braces, no bridges, no caps. If you had a toothache, out came your tooth. When enough of them were missing, the dentist would make you false teeth. By the time they were thirty, both my parents had a full set of choppers, uppers and lowers.

From then on, I tried to make up for lost time, dentally speaking, and brushed regularly; but there would still be lots of fillings and bridges and caps (Oh my!). Now my teeth look almost normal . . . if you don't look too close.

Two other guys from West Virginia were there too. After boot camp, we were all sent to a naval air station in Olathe, Kansas. We were never going to be pilots or mechanics; we were just doing low-level assignments. I got a job at the post office sorting mail.

When my buddies and I would go into Kansas City on liberty for a night, we'd often run into other sailors in bars, and they'd ask what ship we were from. *What ship?* I thought. *Kansas is a helluva long way from any ocean.* As it turned out, these sailors were just home on a two-week leave and had ships to go back to, and we'd have to admit we were just stationed nearby and . . . on land. They'd usually laugh at us and say,

"Oh, you're on the USS Neversail." We felt belittled. We had all joined the Navy to See the World, Sail the Seven Seas, or one sea . . . or a small pond . . . anything.

A few weeks later a notice appeared on a bulletin board in our barracks:

VOLUNTEER FOR SEA DUTY

SIGN UP HERE

This was our big chance! We signed up right away and were flown to California to an island known as Yerba Buena, with the nickname "Goat Island." It was in the middle of Oakland Bay and was referred to as a "repo-depot," which meant we had stopped over there only to be reassigned to our new ships. In no time we were on our way to . . . three different ships . . . never to see one another again.

7
Chipping Rust

So here I was, boarding a ship for the first time. I checked in with the officer of the deck, who looked at my papers and asked what my rank was. I told him "Seaman Second Class, and I'll be working in your mail room." He said, "We've already got someone in our mail room. You'll be working with the deck crew." "What's the deck crew do?" I asked. "Just check in with the bosun's mate," he said.

I was now one of the lowest-of-the-low on the ship. The deck crew seemed like a dead-end job, and it looked like I'd be doing it for a year. Naturally, I was disappointed, but when you're in the service, you just follow orders. The only job the deck crew had was to maintain the deck of the ship, which literally meant chipping rust spots, removing the rust, and repainting it. I soon learned that if you started chipping away rust at the bow of the ship, by the time you finished at the stern you'd have to start all over again on the new rust spots on the bow.

Once in a while, I'd be assigned to work in the scullery, or the kitchen, cleaning up the dinner plates. After the rancid smell of that place, I was happy to get back to chipping rust.

Most of the crew had nicknames. There was Sparky, Tiger, Ducky, and Loverboy. I was just . . . Paul. They had all stenciled their nicknames on their shirt pockets, so I stenciled the name "Rocky" on mine. A guy asked me, "Who's Rocky?" I said, "Oh, that's just my . . . uh . . . my nickname." He said, "Well, you've got some imagination . . . *Paul.*" I finally got it. You can't make up your own nickname; someone's gotta give it to you.

Sailors seemed to love tattoos. Every time they stopped at a new port, they'd get drunk and go to the tattoo parlor. Some of them had six, eight, ten of them. But the record was held by a fifty-year-old career sailor who had sixty-seven tattoos.

One was of a pretty girl inside a heart; there was a tiger, a panther, a snake, and one really scary tattoo . . . "Mother." Above his nipples were the words "hot" and "cold," below them it said "sweet" and "sour." On his forehead was an anchor, on his bald spot an 8-ball, and on his back three sailing ships . . . the *Nina*, the *Pinta*, and the *Santa Maria*. Other tattoos were obviously chosen while drunk and with a weird sense of humor; on his butt cheeks, I swear to God, were rabbit tracks leading to the back end of a bunny disappearing up his butthole. They called him Tattoo John . . . what else?

We had been in port for several months when I was told we were shipping out the next day. Within fifteen minutes of leaving the dock, I was seasick—really, really nauseous.

There I'd be, hanging over the side of the ship, losing my lunch, so when old-timers walked by, they'd say, "What's up, Chuck?" I'd say, "Everything, and my name's not Chuck!" I went to sick bay and told the medic I was seasick and couldn't keep anything down. He said, "Here's an aspirin." I asked, "Is that going to help me?" He said, "Just take it." So, I took it, and guess what? . . . I couldn't keep it down.

See, the Navy's official position on seasickness was "You'll get over it," so you gotta keep doing your job. When I was told I'd be on guard duty, I thought, *It's peacetime, what are they guarding against?* It turned out my guard duty was from two o'clock to six o'clock . . . in the morning. They pointed me to a ladder leading to the crow's nest, which is the tallest point on the ship, and I was pretty sure it was the last place you'd want to be if you were seasick. I was told to sit in the crow's nest with binoculars to see if I could spot any enemy ships.

"What enemy ships?" I asked. I was told, "Don't you know we're having War Games? They started four hours ago. We're the Red Navy, our enemy is the Blue Navy. The games will last three days." For the next four hours I watched for enemy ships, threw up, watched for more ships, threw up, watched some more, and threw up some more and never saw any ships . . . red or blue (my face, by the way, was green).

Finally, relieved of duty, I went back to my bunk and fell asleep. In what seemed like no time I was shaken awake (still nauseous) and told to go clean up the crow's nest. I thought, *Oh, no! Not the crow's nest!* As instructed, I filled a bucket with warm water and soap and started climbing the ladder to the crow's nest. Halfway up, I snapped. I thought, *This is stupid! I'm not gonna go up there again! Not when I'm still sick!* So, I fell off the ladder. Well, I faked falling off the ladder. I was only four steps up so I didn't actually get hurt.

To me, War Games were stupid—a dumb exercise in which grown men pretend to be at war during peacetime. I didn't know it, but behind me on the bridge of the ship, watching everything, were the captain, a visiting admiral, other VIPs, plus the United Press, the Associated Press, and the Newsreels, filming it all. Everyone saw me fall.

I was rushed to the medical office, where I was poked and prodded to find the problem. Still faking it, I said, "No, that doesn't hurt," and "Yes, that hurts a little" in a random kind of way until finally it was decided I had a ruptured appendix.

The officers were very excited. Here they had a real crisis during a pretend war. Since the problem couldn't be handled by the medics on our ship, they decided to transfer me to another ship, an aircraft carrier, where they had a surgeon. I thought, *Wait a minute, a surgeon? But there's nothing wrong with me. I'm just . . .* and then it hit me, in all the excitement, I was no longer seasick, just terrified of being found out, and for what? Lying to the authorities? About a "phantom pain?" Since my offense happened kinda during a war, was it treason? What would my punishment be? Would I have to "walk the plank"? Or go "under the lash"? Of the two, I thought . . . *I'll take the lash.*

I was now brought out on deck and strapped onto a metal stretcher, which would be attached to a cable leading to the other ship.

I was hoisted aloft to begin my journey into War Games history. The ships were about fifty yards apart. I was strapped in tight, so I couldn't fall out. The cable was taut, the sea was choppy, and if my ship zigged when the other ship zagged and the cable snapped, I'd be plunged into the ocean and be sleeping with the fishes. I was scared. I wondered, *Is it too late to call it off?* But I figured, *No. I'm in over my head now . . . so to speak.*

After what seemed like a lifetime, I was aboard the aircraft carrier, and once again I was examined by doctors. This time, I downplayed my symptoms and was put under observation for two hours. After that, since I was doing well (surprise, surprise!), they extended my observation four more hours. Finally, they only checked on me overnight.

The aircraft carrier was quite near Honolulu, Hawaii. The next day I saw a local newspaper with a picture of me crossing between two ships. My parents' names and their address were listed below it. Apparently, the Associated Press article was everywhere. I was afraid my parents would be worried, but I was able to call them (ship-to-shore phone) and explain that it was just a false alarm and I was okay. Another day of this, and I was *miraculously* back to normal. Calling my case a misdiagnosis, I was returned to my ship. When I got there, all my shipmates were lined up applauding me and taking pictures; I was sort of a "War Games hero," a "celebrity." It was great, but I hadn't earned their approval and felt guilty about my "big lie."

At that time, Hollywood sent all the new movies to the Army, the Navy, and the Marines. Our ship had a big screen, and that night, when my shipmates and I went to see the newest movie, there was a Mickey Mouse cartoon . . . and the newsreels of the War Games, some of them on our very own ship. I actually saw myself being strapped into my stretcher and courageously crossing the ocean blue. I have to say, I seemed pretty convincing. At that moment I had a crazy thought. *Could it be . . . that I might have a future as an actor?* And now . . . for the Best Performance by a Seasick Sailor . . . Me!

I never got over being seasick, but I did get used to it. It usually lasted for only two or three days after leaving port, then I'd feel okay. They called that "Getting your Sea Legs," but each time we were *in port* for even a few days and then went back to sea, it happened all over again. By the way, a seagoing ship goes very, very slowly. It took us four weeks to go from Oakland to Japan, then on to China and Hawaii. Those are very nice places, but all I remember about the Navy is . . . throwing up and chipping rust.

One thing I did take away from the Navy was a good joke:

> A new recruit on his first day aboard ship was put to
> work. After an hour he reported to his superior. He
> said, "Excuse me, Sir? I finished mopping the floor,
> can I go downstairs now?" His foreman exploded,
> *"Mopping the floor? Go downstairs?* Look, Buddy,
> you're in the *Navy* now! You don't *mop the floor!* You
> *swab the deck*! It's not *downstairs*, it's *below deck*! This
> is *topside*! That's *port*! That's starboard! In the Navy,
> *everything's got its own name.* If I *ever* hear you say
> '*mop the floor*' again, I'm gonna throw you out that
> . . . little . . . round . . . window over there!"

~

February 1948. I'm out of the Navy, twenty years old, all grown up, and glad to be home. I had gotten my "mustering out" pay of two hundred dollars. I went to the best men's store in town, bought a new double-breasted midnight-blue suit, a new pair of two-toned shoes, a dress shirt, cuff links, and three neckties.

I hung them in the closet and never found an occasion to wear them again.

I still got together with my old gang, but we didn't seem to be as carefree as we once were. They all had returned to their factory jobs, so I went back to work at Universal Glass . . . at least for the time being.

With great expectations, I went to the river. The place was a ghost of what it had been. The swing was gone, taken down or fallen off somehow. The biggest change was that the river was now six feet higher. The roots of the giant oak tree were underwater. My brother explained that a series of locks had been installed farther up the river to control water levels during spring flooding.

Years later, I read Thomas Wolfe's book *You Can't Go Home Again*. He was right.

Then something happened that would change the course of my life. I ran into Jim Dukas downtown one day, and he asked what my plans were. I told him, "I don't really have any. What about you?" "I'm going to college at WVU, why don't you join me?" he said. "I don't wanna be no college boy," I told him. I had no idea what I meant by that; no one in my family had even finished high school. "Besides," I said, "isn't it kind of expensive?" He laughed. "You don't have to pay to get in. You're a Vet, you've got the GI Bill; they'll pay your tuition and give you a monthly check to live on."

I wasn't sure I wanted to go to college; maybe more scared than anything. Jim said, "Well, I'm majoring in theater with a minor in art. I'm doing plays, I'm painting, cartooning, and working evenings at the local radio station." "Do you think I could even get in?" I asked. "Are you kidding?" he said. "Half the students there are Vets. Why not give it a year? We could even shoot some silent movies. . . . What do you think?" I hesitated. Then he said, "You know, the place is full of young girls away from home for the first time." And I thought to myself, *This college thing is sounding better and better.*

In the fall I started classes at West Virginia University in Morgantown, West Virginia. As a freshman, I found that my classmates, like me, liked jokes. Now I could share my jokes with them. They even had a few new jokes, and by that I mean, old jokes I had never heard.

> The hotel room was so small, when you put the key
> in the door . . . you broke the window.

> The room service was so bad . . . the mice went out
> to eat.

8
Don't Call It Theater

My classes would include Acting, Directing, Dialects, and History of the Theater. Okay, I could *study* Theater, but I couldn't *call* it that. Instead, I studied "Speech" in the "Speech" Department. Theater seemed to be too "artsy" for the university. After all, what were the odds that any of these students, including me, would ever become professional actors? As a "Speech" student, I had to also study Voice and Diction, Argumentation, and Debate.

Teaching students how to speak properly was going to be quite a task since nearly all the student body had West Virginia accents. Instead, the goal was to train them to speak well enough for a business meeting, or at the Elks Club, the Eagle's Club, or a funeral.

Many of the teachers had attended WVU, had studied "Speech," had graduated, then had come back to teach there. I wasn't sure, but it seemed to me that they sounded a lot like me, and I certainly had a bit of an accent myself. Of course, I came by it honestly. My whole family, my parents, and especially my grandparents, had a strong accent, but having spent two years in the Navy around a lot of other people, my own accent had changed somewhat . . . thinned out a little.

Just a word about the accent: West Virginia has a sound that's not quite Southern and not quite Northern but still very strange. For example, the word "bush" comes out as "boosh," a "dish" is a "deesh," "wash" is "warsh," "special" becomes "spatial," "tires" are "tars," and so on. When I went to work at age sixteen for Universal Glass, I was told to go see Shorty Wilson. I asked, "Who's Shorty Wilson?" and was told, "Oh, he's the guy who 'hars and fars'" (obviously the personnel manager).

~

A prerequisite to be a "Speech" major was that every student would need to make a recording of his voice reading a selection of some sort. I chose the poem "Abou Ben Adhem."

The recording, by the way, was not on *tape*; instead, a *wire* recorder was used. That's right. A piece of wire onto which a one-minute recording could be made.

Four years later, a week before graduation, I was required to record the same selection again. It would then be compared to the original reading and progress evaluated. I must have done well since I received my diploma. As a souvenir, they gave me both recordings.

Later, living in New York, I'd forgotten all about the wire recordings; I just wasn't interested. One day I was telling a friend about them, and he said, "I'd like to hear them." I said, "So would I." I had never listened to them. I found them in the back of my closet and played them. In the first part, recorded in 1948, I sounded like the hillbilly I was then. I played the 1952 version (four years later, after all my "Speech" training), and I sounded . . . exactly the same. I mean *exactly*. We both had to laugh.

After six months in the city, without any help from my college "Speech" training, I had lost my accent. I could only figure that I had listened to radio announcers, TV announcers, and actors in movies and on TV and imitated them.

Jim Dukas and I continued making silent films around campus, and Bob Lichello, my buddy from high school, joined us. He was in college now too. Bob and I were living on the GI Bill with a $66 a month allotment. To save money, we decided to room together. We looked for the cheapest place we could find. It was in a small village about a mile away from campus by bus. As a wannabe actor, I loved my new address: Star City, West Virginia (if only the street had been named Broadway). We each paid five dollars a week for one room with two beds, and breakfast and dinner were thrown in. Not a bad deal.

9
Tastes Like Chicken

Our landlady, Mrs. Jones, raised rabbits. Flemish Giants, they were called. Nearly every night for dinner we'd have what she called *chicken*. We all knew it was *rabbit*. The drumsticks were the size of turkey legs (it was rabbit alright!). Bob and I expected at any moment it would hop off the plate. After dinner we would amuse each other by naming the meal we just had; was it "Rabbit a la King?" "Kentucky Fried Rabbit?" or maybe even "Bunny Bolognese?" Which is either a delicious Italian dish . . . or a Mafia wife.

As many rabbits as we ate, the rabbit population in the pens out back never seemed to change. We could only assume that they were reproducing like . . . well, rabbits.

Lichello was a journalism major and made extra money by entering contests. The nearest big-city newspaper was in Pittsburgh. Their weekend edition had a contest where readers would send in a short letter answering the question of the week. Bob studied these letters and figured out how they picked the winners. Every week, he sent in a letter, usually from a housewife with a fake name. He would also add a folksy bit of down-home humor. He always won first or second prize, sometimes both, for either ten or five dollars.

I don't know how he got away with it, but I do know he had a post office box where he got mail, and he had given them a list of his fake names. I was never sure how he got paid. I think, maybe, they just put a five- or a ten-dollar bill in an envelope. Why they didn't catch on to the fact that many, many winners had the same post office box in Morgantown, West Virginia, is a mystery. He was quite a con man.

Lichello also sold a story to *STAG*, a men's magazine, about my misadventure in the Navy. He called it "Hoax on the High Seas" and changed my name to protect my privacy. They paid him twenty-five dollars (and I didn't even get a dime out of it).

~

The university library was a treasure trove. I discovered a lot more about Keaton. It turns out he had started in vaudeville. *But what the heck was that?* Well, forget about my classes, I started to study vaudeville!

Keaton was born into the family business. His parents traveled the country doing a "Knockabout" act full of tumbling and pratfalls. At the age of four, he wandered onstage and was such a hit he became a part of the act: "The Three Keatons." Soon, he even got a salary.

The kid was thrown around the stage like a bowling ball. His father even attached the handle of a suitcase to his costume, all the better to toss him around. He learned to take falls the hard way. Speaking of falling down and not getting hurt, Keaton once said, "When a little kid falls down, he doesn't have far to go."

His dad saw that when his son fell down and didn't react it was funnier, so he taught him never to smile. Once, when he was very young, he accidentally fell down a flight of stairs and walked away unhurt. A fellow performer said, "That was quite a buster." That's how he got his name. That man was Harry Houdini, the Handcuff King. I noticed that even Buster had a nickname.

At that time, young children weren't allowed to perform onstage, so his dad—not the father of the year—taught him to smoke a cigar and passed him off as a midget.

About the time I was born, vaudeville was kind of fading out. A year later, vaudeville was on its last legs . . . and I was just learning to walk. The more I found out about vaudeville, the more I was drawn to it. It was like something I was meant to do but born too late to be a part of.

The library also had a collection of Keaton's feature films, all considered classics, some even masterpieces. In a period of five years, he had created nine of them; I could now finally see *The General, The Navigator, Sherlock Junior, Steamboat Bill,* and all the others.

Not only was Keaton a genius as a comedian, but he is also considered a pioneering filmmaker. He experimented with the medium, finding innovative ways of using the camera. He has been referred to as the "Architect of Silent Comedy."

In his book *The Silent Clowns*, Walter Kerr, the *New York Times* drama critic (and I'm paraphrasing here) referred to silent pictures and radio as two "perfect art forms," because silent pictures, without speech, allowed the audience to participate in the story by imagining their own words, and radio invited its listeners to create their own pictures. Oddly enough, I was hooked on both of them.

~

For class, I needed to choose a foreign language. I picked Italian. My friend Lichello took it too (he was already Italian). Our teacher, Mr. Simonetti, was a very nice, somewhat stout, real Italian. For the first two weeks I was doing very well; Lichello was grilling me in the evening to help me memorize words. After class one day, the teacher asked me if there were Italians in my family. I told him there weren't. He said, "That's strange because your accent is very good." This surprised me, because I was pretty sure my own accent was pure West Virginia. Nearly all the students spoke the same way; it was, after all, a state university. In class I seemed to be pronouncing the Italian words properly, while I could hear my classmates butchering the vocabulary with their accents, which made it sound funny to me.

Mr. Simonetti and I were both still puzzled by the way I picked up the accent. Then it came to me. I was just imitating the teacher. Looking back on it now, I realize that, just as musicians have an *ear* for music, so most actors have an *ear* for dialects.

At the end of the semester my grade was an A, so I signed up for Italian 2. The next semester when I had an elective class, again I chose

Italian. And the next semester, and the next. Finally, I switched my minor from Art to Italian. After two years, I was fluent, then, my classes consisted of Conversation in Italian, Italian History, Italian Literature (we read *Dante's Inferno* in Italian). My grades were all A's. I began to feel Italian. I thought maybe in a previous life I had lived in Italy.

Much later, I visited Italy several times, and even though I saw Rome, Venice, and Naples, the city I fell in love with was Florence. There was the Ponte Vecchio, a bridge over the River Arno, with many, many quaint little shops selling anything and everything to tourists. Best of all, there was the museum featuring Michelangelo's *David*. It was something beautiful to behold. I beholded it three times.

~

I had only two teachers at WVU who were important to me as an actor. The first was an older woman, beautiful and dignified, and years earlier she had been a well-known Broadway actress who had worked for the legendary David Belasco. Her name was Marja Fear. She taught a course in "Oral Interpretation," the art of revealing the undercurrents and motivations of dialogue. I learned more about how to speak on stage from her than from anyone else. She was outstanding!

The other teacher was Sam Boyd, who taught dialects. He had been a professional actor in New York, specializing in accents on radio shows. I learned from Sam that dialects come about when groups from other countries come to, for example, the United States, and live near each other in large cities, and over time they influence each other's way of speaking . . . in other words, a new accent. Sam told us that the New York City accent was a blending of Irish, Italian, and Jewish. Of course, that was in the 1950s. Now, the accent might reflect more Hispanic speech, and other groups who have come to be part of the mix.

Long after college, dialects still fascinated me. It would seem that doing an accent would mean changing every word. Actually, it's mostly the vowels that need to be changed, as many consonants are the same in all languages (the K, the M, the P, for example). There is one exception.

The letter R is unique. In many, many languages the R sound is very different. In Spanish and Italian, the R is rolled . . . "RR." In Scotland, it's also rolled . . . "RRR." In the United Kingdom, the R is silent. Car becomes "cah." In Boston, New York, and even down South, car is "cah," a soft R, and in the Midwest the R is really sounded out, becoming a hard R. Asians use L in place of an R, the French R sounds more nasal, the German R more guttural, and so on.

~

I got to know the very funny Don Knotts at college. Everyone else got to know him much later as the bumbling deputy Barney Fife on *The Andy Griffith Show*. He was also the landlord on TV's *Three's Company* and could be seen in a handful of Disney comedies with Tim Conway.

Don had started performing comedy in high school with a ventriloquist dummy and continued doing that in college. He was then drafted into the Army. Don's experience as an entertainer got him assigned to a unit called "Special Services," where he spent the next two years entertaining soldiers. He never carried a gun and never dug a foxhole. He just did comedy routines at Army camps all over the country. A pretty sweet assignment during a war. By the time Don left the Army and went back to WVU for his senior year, he had become a polished, professional comedian . . . with just a trace of an accent.

Don Knotts, later to become Barney Fife. CBS/ PHOTOFEST ©CBS

I began to spend more time with Don. On a couple of weekends, we drove to Pittsburgh to see a burlesque show. No one at school would believe we went there to see the comics. "Yeah, sure," they'd say. "You don't want to see the strippers. Oh no!" To be honest, we found the strippers boring. On the drive back to school, Don and I would reconstruct the sketches since they were fresh in our minds. What I didn't remember, he'd remember. Later we'd perform the routines, which were kind of bawdy, just for fraternities.

He also taught me my first magic trick: disappearing a quarter. I practiced for hours in front of a mirror until I got it right. I graduated from coins to balls, cigarettes, and cards. I still practice sleight of hand . . . I've even been known to make an entire chocolate cake disappear.

~

When I was in my second year of college, TV started becoming a thing. Very few people had TV sets, and certainly no college students. At that time, you'd have to go to a bar to see a TV show. Soon all that changed. Everyone was talking about *The Milton Berle Show*. He was a fast-talking comedian, and his show was so popular people started running out to buy TV sets. The Berle show was a phenomenon. TV sales went through the roof. Other comedians were jealous of Berle's success. One of them, George Jessel, said:

> "Milton Berle is responsible for selling more TV sets
> than anyone. I sold mine . . . my uncle sold his . . .
> my cousin . . ."

Berle's was a variety show: lots of comedy, lots of celebrity guests, and vaudeville acts of all kinds. He was famous for stealing jokes. They called him the "Thief of Bad Gags."

As much as I loved comedy, I hated Milton Berle. He was brash and obnoxious and would do anything for a laugh. He had no taste. In the wake of Berle's success, came two genuine masters of comedy: Sid Caesar and Jackie Gleason. They both had variety shows, but, unlike Berle, they had style and class and were easily four times as funny. With Caesar, the word "comic genius" comes to mind. It's the same with Gleason. Buster was still number one, but I also loved those two guys.

As a comic actor, Sid Caesar could do anything. He was great at pantomime and could do double-talk in any foreign language. He sharpened his skills at a summer resort, Camp Tamiment in the Pocono Mountains of Pennsylvania, and went on to star in early TV on *Your Show of Shows*. There were no guest stars, just Caesar and his gang—a pert little pixie named Imogene Coca, his very versatile straight man Carl Reiner, and scrappy character actor Howard Morris, all accomplished sketch actors. Together, they were like a three-ring circus. Caesar's talent, and his explosive energy, caused the show to take off like a comic juggernaut.

His show also had the greatest group of comedy writers ever assembled. There was Neil Simon, later the king of Broadway comedies (more than thirty of them, including *The Odd Couple*), Larry Gelbart, who created TV's *M*A*S*H*, Mel Brooks, a young Woody Allen, and others. They are, to this day, all comedy legends.

Jackie Gleason is most well-known as the bombastic Ralph Kramden on *The Honeymooners*, but there was much more to him than that. In his early TV career, there was *The Jackie Gleason Show*. Not a variety show with guest stars; Gleason was the whole show. He appeared in short character sketches, all of them completely different. He was loudmouth Joe the Bartender, the Poor Soul, a lovable loser who never spoke, and Reginald Van Gleason III, a vain, hard-drinking rich guy. He later added Art Carney as his clueless sidekick. There was never another team like them. Gleason was light on his feet, a graceful fat man, and under all that comic talent, he was a great actor . . . just watch the film *The Hustler* and see for yourself.

In 1951, when I was a junior in college, while watching Caesar and Gleason I realized something. Since I couldn't be a silent comedian and

found acting in plays not right for me, I knew what I wanted to be was
. . . a sketch actor. That type of comedy was just a little bigger and a
little funnier than play acting.

I also tried to imagine what name I might use if I really became a
sketch comic someday. I wanted something that would *sound* funny
so that audiences hearing it would expect *me* to be funny. Here are
two names that I actually . . . stupidly considered; "Buster Brown" and
"Tom Foolery."

~

I was doing cartoons for the college humor magazine, signing them
with my initials, PB. When I did cartoons just for myself, I experimented with other names. I found Irish names had more of a comic
sound to me. I'd sign a cartoon O'Connor or Kelly, and I liked the
name Muldoon. My favorite name was Dooley. A couple of times the
local high school asked the university to send some actors to perform
at their annual fair. I volunteered, dressed as a clown, and called myself
Dooley.

~

You may have noticed that all my life I've loved jokes, collecting them,
and sometimes, telling them but never ever thinking I could invent
anything funny . . . until one moment in college.

The theater students had a lounge where we socialized. Once, for a
party, somebody made up a Halloween-themed fake menu . . . Ghoul
Soup, Ghost Beef, and Wicked Waffles. A little lame, but it did give me
an idea. I had a class in Abnormal Psychology that delved into sadism
and masochism. I created a masochist menu:

Club Steak

Mashed Potatoes

Black-Eyed-Peas
Beets

Devil's Food Cake
with Whipped Cream

Punch

10
Loretta

To go back a bit to when I was a college freshman . . . I found that, because I hadn't had Algebra in high school, I was required to take it in college. I was having a hard time and just couldn't seem to get it. After a few classes, we were told there would be a test the next day. A fellow student, Loretta, could see I was struggling with the class and took pity on me. (Her name has been changed to protect her privacy . . . and if this book turns out to be terrible, I may change my name too.)

Loretta and I went to a coffee shop where she talked me through what the quiz would likely cover; I passed the test. We became friends and through the semester she helped me pass Algebra with a C. I was grateful, and we kept in touch.

A guy from Algebra class asked me later if Loretta and I were "going together." I said, "No, she's just a friend." He told me, "Everyone in class thought you were a couple." I thought, *Oh, that's why she was being so nice to me.* I guess I was a little slow on the uptake.

I started seeing her more often and began to appreciate who she was. She was very attractive and also very smart. She worked as a secretary for the president of the university for just four hours a day, and the rest of the time she was in class. She was local and lived at home with her family. She was eighteen, I was twenty. We were obviously attracted to each other, but after class she'd go straight home. Her parents were very strict, very Italian, and very, very Catholic.

It was hard for us to find the time, or the place, to be alone. At the Speech Department, there was a large theater. Rehearsals for plays were usually in the evenings, and the theater was often empty during the day.

There were spaces above the stage where scenery and lights were hung. We would climb a ladder, find a dark spot on the catwalk, and "neck" (1940s talk for making out). We were both very turned on (1940s talk for hot), and for five or ten minutes we'd be all over each other, but she would never go "all the way" (and certainly not on a catwalk). I was very frustrated, and, as I said, she was not only Catholic ... but also a virgin. We were together, while apart, for quite a while. Later, she took an evening class, and we'd go to a park afterwards for half an hour. Finally, she gave in, and we "did it." This didn't happen often.

One day she missed her classes, and a friend of hers at work told me she was out sick. That evening she managed to call me. She had been feeling weird for a while, and then she missed her period. Still an innocent, she went to the family doctor, who immediately called her parents to say she was pregnant. All hell broke loose. She confessed it all to them and told them who I was, and her father told her to call me and tell me to come over to their house ... *Now!*

On the phone, in tears, she told me, "You have to come over here." I, for sure, didn't want to get married, much less, have a baby. Desperate, and hoping I wouldn't die at her father's hands, I improvised. "Here's what you do, confess that we are also secretly married. If your father wants proof, tell him I've got the marriage certificate, but that I'm away for the weekend visiting my parents, and on Monday I'll bring over the certificate."

We both skipped classes on Monday, went to City Hall, and got married. Loretta, cleverly, changed the date on the marriage license at her office and finally, I met the family. Scandal, and possibly death, averted!

I was kicking myself for how stupid I had been. We had had sex only a few times. I had used protection, but in the heat of the moment, I must have, at least once, forgot.

I started looking for an apartment, and she stayed at home with her parents. Then one day she called to tell me she'd lost the baby. She had had a little fall. I said, "You don't mean ... on purpose?" "No. It just happened." I believed her, but I would never quite know the real story. I had married her so that her family could save face . . . but also to give our maybe-baby a name.

So here we were, married, never having dated and never having said "I love you." I found a small apartment and our life together began. I can't say I didn't enjoy it; after all, I liked her very much, she liked me, and we could even speak Italian together.

We settled in, and it was actually pretty nice. She made meals for us (lots of pasta), and we had friends over. Being the only married couple in our group, our single friends would hang out at our place. I had my check from the government, and her small salary helped. We were doing alright.

We both knew this was not a regular marriage. We agreed to keep it going until we graduated, and then we'd go to New York City as we had both planned. If we wanted to stay married, we would. If not, well . . . maybe not.

We made it through that first year. I took the summer break to be with my family. While there, I also spent time with my old gang and did some freelance cartoons for my hometown paper. Loretta, who still had her job in the president's office, took some summer classes, stayed in our apartment, and spent more time with her parents, who had cautiously begun to accept our situation.

That summer, when I was just twenty-one, I came across a new issue of *LIFE* magazine. It had a lengthy article on the four great silent movie comedians (Chaplin, Keaton, Harold Lloyd, and Harry Langdon). The article was written by famous screenwriter, novelist, and film critic James Agee.

It was an in-depth analysis of their characters and their art. Although I knew a lot about them, that article inspired me and told me even more. It became my bible, and I have the cover framed in my office.

When silent films came along there was a great demand for actors who could tell stories without words and comedians who could be funny without talking. They came from theater, from vaudeville, even the circus. Clowns, tumblers, acrobats, mimes, anyone who could take a fall, take a pie in the face, or a kick in the pants was perfect for silent comedy.

Many of these early comics were good at the knockabout style but never became stars. That all changed with Chaplin. In 1914 he was hired by Mack Sennett for Keystone Films. When he began, he was paid $150 a week.

After only a handful of short films, his popularity began to grow. He started to direct his own pictures. Audiences were going crazy for his movies. He soon eclipsed all other comedians. He was a phenomenon, whose face was known all over the world.

By 1915, Chaplin signed a new contract for $1,250 a week, with a $10,000 bonus for signing.

In 1916, he signed a contract for $670,000 for the year.

In 1928, Chaplin joined Mary Pickford and Douglas Fairbanks, two of Hollywood's biggest stars, and director D. W. Griffith to create their own studio, United Artists, and could now control the profits from their work.

Chaplin was comedy royalty, and if he was the king, Keaton was the prince. There was also Harold Lloyd (the man hanging from the giant clock) and baby-faced Harry Langdon, who was considered fourth among the "Big Four" of silent clowns, but I consider him to be number three. I never cared for Harold Lloyd, who was certainly very popular, and even though he was funny, for me his character lacked the artistry of the others.

Langdon's persona was that of a four-year-old child. He had a baby face, pursed lips, and innocent eyes, and his moves were always hesitant. The best of Harry Langdon is awfully good.

I've seen all their films, shorts, and features. You could say I majored in Silent Comedy History and have followed it ever since.

~

There were two other heroes of mine doing comedy when movies could finally speak. First and foremost were Stan Laurel and Oliver Hardy, the funniest, and most endearing, of all screen comedians. They still used lots of pantomime, and their voices now matched their characters. They were the only comedy team who ever seemed to like each other.

My other favorite was the irascible W. C. Fields, who liked nobody . . . but made me laugh.

11

The Lost Private

The next summer, a fellow student was hired as a scenic designer at a summer theater in Pennsylvania. He recommended me to work there as an apprentice. I would help paint scenery, hang lights, pull curtains, and play small parts with a company of professional actors. We did ten shows in ten weeks, and I learned more about theater that summer than college ever taught me.

As I said, I played only small parts. I was fine with that. It was enough for me to be part of it all, working with those professional actors and getting twenty-five dollars a week.

As the director got to know me better, he told me our next play would be *At War with the Army*, a sort of "gang" comedy. He said, "I've already cast all the leads, but there are a lot of smaller parts, some of them pretty funny. Take a look at the script and pick out a part you'd like to play." One part jumped out to me. There were no lines; the character never spoke. I thought, *I can do something with this!*

The play was set in an office at an Army camp. There were a lot of desks and lots of activity; soldier's running in and out of doors constantly . . . a typical farce. In that office was a giant Coke machine. Every soldier who tried to buy a Coke lost his nickel. This went on and on. The soldiers bitched about it and the audience laughed at it. The Coke machine had become another character in the play.

Suddenly, outside the office, two Jeeps were in a fender bender and all the soldiers ran outside to see what had happened . . . the stage was empty.

That's when I made my entrance.

The character was billed as "The Lost Private" . . . and he was very lost. It was obviously his first day in the Army. I chose the costume: My pants were too big, my shirt was too long, my helmet was oversized. On my back was a knapsack, a shovel, a canteen, and a rifle; I was ladened down. I held in my hand my official papers. I wandered in and around the desks, offering my papers to invisible clerks. Finding none, I decide to leave. As I get to the door, I take one look back and I see the Coke machine.

Until then I was getting titters, then chuckles, but when they saw me discover the Coke machine, that's when the big laughs really started (and it only got better from there).

I went to the Coke machine to get a Coke, but first I had to take off all my gear, and then I put my nickel in the machine and waited . . . and waited. Nothing. I had lost my nickel. The audience was eating it up. The machine and I were now a comedy team.

Disappointed, I put my gear back on, piece by piece, and headed for the door again . . . but just as I got there, I heard a "clunk." My coin had been returned. I went back to get the money. I picked up my nickel and turned away for a moment. Six more nickels dropped. As I was retrieving them, ten more nickels came down. I took my helmet off to catch them all.

Finally, I foolishly put one last nickel in, just to see what would happen. The machine said, "Moo" and a bottle of milk came out. Curtain. Wild applause.

I later learned that when *At War with the Army* played on Broadway, the actor playing the Lost Private stole the show . . . and so did I . . . (or was it that Coke machine?).

Sometimes I think of those *six minutes* onstage and realize that, *in all my work over the next sixty-five years*, I have never been *that good, that perfect* for a part, nor enjoyed acting more in my life.

My ace in the hole was that I was playing silent movie comic Harry Langdon . . . not as his baby-faced character . . . but just as an innocent, clown-like soldier.

The following year Bob Lichello and I formed a comedy team and began to get bookings around town at the Elks Club, the Eagle's Club, the Moose Club, and places like that. We did nothing but old jokes and were probably not very funny. We never made more than ten dollars a night, split two ways, but we were having fun.

Of the many plays I did in college, one stands out. It was a comedy called *Harvey*. I played a man who could see a six-foot-tall white rabbit named Harvey that no one else could see (Jimmy Stewart played the part in the movie). It was one of my favorite roles. Later, I played it several times in summer theaters.

The university never played favorites; every student was given a chance in the spotlight. However, the Student Theatre Group created their own shows and could cast anyone they liked. I played the comedy leads in all their musicals . . . even though I could barely sing.

~

For a long time, I'd been obsessed with jokes. I wanted to learn more about the mechanics, the inner workings of jokes. In my senior year of college, I thought I had figured something out. I asked my professor if, instead of writing my thesis, I could do a live presentation. He asked, "What would your topic be?" I said, "My theory of comedy." He said, "That sounds interesting. Okay, we'll have the whole class listen to it." I knew that a lecture on comedy could actually become boring, so I sprinkled in enough humorous examples to make it fun for the class.

I already knew there was a "Rule of Three" in comedy; I wanted to explore it. A huge number of jokes can be explained by "1-2-change." But why is that?

This was my theory. Two is the minimum number of examples needed to establish a pattern that will then be broken (one is two few . . . four is too many). The third step is the variation, the joke, the punch line. I am certainly not the first person to think of this, nearly every comedian and every joke writer would know it; but at twenty-four, I thought I was inventing the wheel.

At last, Loretta and I graduated. We had always gotten along well, and we were very compatible. Still, we never talked about our agreement or our future.

~

In June of 1952 Loretta and I headed for New York with just $50 between us. That seems like nothing now, but things were cheaper then. Today, that would be over $400. I was driving a 1946 Dodge given to us by her father. We were young, fearless, maybe even a little naive, and so excited to get to Broadway and 42nd Street . . . nothing could stop us.

True to our "understanding," she checked into a cheap hotel and I took a room at the YMCA for five dollars a week. Within hours we realized we desperately missed each other (so much for being independent). We had our meals together, and naturally I'd stay with her for a few hours in the evenings. When I'd leave later the desk clerk would give me a strange look for being in the room with my own wife.

It didn't take long to realize that owning a car in the city was a liability. I sold that 1946 Dodge and thereafter took the subway.

~

Right away we looked for jobs. Loretta soon landed a pretty good position in the garment district. She would be a showroom model. After all, Loretta was pretty and had a nice figure. I was not that pretty, and I don't think I even had a figure.

I found a minimum-wage job; it paid a whopping seventy-five cents an hour. Since, in the Navy, I had been sorting mail, my new job would be at a publishing house . . . sorting mail. It was not a demanding job— all I needed to know was the alphabet.

Loretta found her new job exciting. It was a little like show business. All day long she'd model bathing suits for out-of-town buyers who then selected items to order for their department stores around the country.

My new job was repetitive and mind-numbing, I sorted letters based on which state they were from. I found that the names on the return addresses were often kind of interesting and sometimes sort of funny.

There were a dozen people sorting. I was probably the fastest, but every time I saw a name I liked I would stop and write it down. A month later I was called into the boss's office. I thought, *Maybe I'll get a raise to . . . I don't know, eighty cents an hour?* There was no raise. Instead, I was told that an efficiency expert had been clocking our work and found that I was the slowest of all the sorters; I was fired. This was sixty-five years ago, but I still have the list, and those forty names still intrigue me.

Some of the names were very quaint, often going back for centuries . . . Mary Bytheway, John Wellborn, Lester Easterday. I feel it's okay now to share these names with you. I don't think I will be subject to a class-action suit from medieval England.

Some names, on the other hand, just made me smile . . . Waldo Letzlaff, Eber Goostree, Billy Buckalew, and Lulu Jelly.

~

In college I had been encouraged by my teachers to try New York. One of them confided in me, "You know, you're the best actor in your class." I soon found out that every best actor in his class was in the city now, and they were all my competition.

At the university, although there were classes in acting, oddly, we never learned anything about the business of being a professional actor. I barely knew what an agent was . . . or that I would certainly need one. I knew for sure I'd need professional pictures, so I got them.

I also knew I needed a résumé listing the plays I'd done in college (although, in New York, nobody cared what you'd done in college).

An actor told me, "Just 'pad' your résumé, you know, list a few shows with a lot of actors in them like ... *South Pacific, The Caine Mutiny,* or *12 Angry Men.* Nobody will know the difference." So, I padded my résumé. I mean, I *really* padded it, like I was gonna sleep on it.

I would also need a phone service, a number I could list on my résumé where potential employers might leave me a

My first professional picture . . . stand back, ladies! PHOTOFEST

message (there were no cell phones yet). I found a service for $3.50 a month, and for many, many months I never got a single message. As an actor, I was still on the outside looking in.

I began to "make the rounds," going door to door meeting agents (or their receptionists). Of course, an agent is never going to sign you as a client without ever seeing your work, so it was kind of pointless, but that's how you got started ... maybe even taking a part as an extra (a nonspeaking role) on some TV show.

I was broke most of the time, so lunch at the Automat, where everything was paid for with nickels from a sort-of vending machine, would be Franks and Beans for just fifteen cents, or three nickels, and if I wanted to really go crazy, once in a while I'd stop at Chock Full o' Nuts and get a cream cheese on date nut bread sandwich and chicken noodle soup for about thirty cents.

Most successful actors are good at promoting themselves. I was not. I knew I had talent but hoped that my work would get me work, and in the end it did ... but it took quite a while.

Making the rounds was so depressing that I would sometimes just play hooky and watch the McCarthy hearings on TV. Senator Joseph

McCarthy was a corrupt senator, a demagogue on a witch hunt for "*communists.*" His lawyer was the infamous Roy Cohn. It was riveting television; I could not stop watching it.

In all this, there was one bright spot. The networks did not yet have a system in place to find audiences for their live shows. I can remember ushers from the networks out on the street handing out tickets to shows . . . for free! I got to see many of the Sid Caesar shows . . . *live*, and they were great!

~

After three months in the city without any work as an actor, I was about ready to give up. I couldn't get a job, couldn't get an agent, I couldn't get arrested. I felt like a real . . .

los·er

/ˈloozər/

noun

A person who is incompetent or unable to succeed.

That sounds like who I am . . . at least for now.

12
Second Acting

When an out-of-work actor can't afford a ticket to a Broadway show, he joins the crowd on the sidewalk at intermission, then casually saunters back inside and finds an empty seat. It's called Second Acting. I saw quite a few plays that way, but just the second act, of course, which could be confusing. Sometimes I'd put two second acts together to make one show, like . . .

A Streetcar Named Oklahoma

or *Fiddler on the Gypsy*

and I loved *My Fair Lady Macbeth*

There was always a chance of getting caught and asked to leave. Since I wasn't doing any "real acting," I decided to become an expert at "second acting" and use my acting skills to get away with it. Once I was in the theater, I'd wait until the lights started to dim and find an empty seat. Sometimes an usher would come over and say . . .

"May I see your ticket please?"
"Well, you got me. Actually, I *have* a ticket, but I was in the balcony, and I noticed there were empty seats down here, so . . . ya know what, I'll go back up to the balcony."
"No, no. You're here now. Just stay."

Maybe I was a pretty good actor . . . or a pretty good liar.

Once, I asked an actress, both of us out of work, "You want to second-act a play with me?" She said, "I guess so." Once we were inside, standing in the back, she got cold feet. She said, "What if someone wants to see our tickets?" I think I wanted to impress her, so I picked up a program, leafed through it, and said, "You see this? House Manager: Norman Freedman. If anyone asks, I'll say I'm a friend of his." Sure enough, someone did ask.

"May I see your ticket, please?"
"I'm a friend of Norman Freedman."
"I'm Norman Freedman."
"Oh. Hi, Norman. Remember me?"

He must have had a good sense of humor, because he just laughed and said . . . "Get out!"

～

Loretta and I continued to see each other (after all, we *were married*, and she was still my best friend . . . my only friend). At dinner one night, she told me she had found an apartment but was not sure she could afford the rent. She asked me, "Would you consider sharing it with me? I could pay the rent and you could buy the groceries. What do you think?" I was still at the YMCA and still lonely. I hadn't met anyone else, and it was just a one-year lease, so I said, "Sure."

The apartment was on 25th Street in the Chelsea neighborhood and was fairly new. It seemed to be just right for us. We bought a bed, moved in, and slowly began to furnish the place.

Loretta was soon promoted. No longer a showroom model, she was now a stylist for Jantzen bathing suits. She traveled a lot, going to major department stores around the country, producing and narrating fashion shows with local models. She enjoyed it very much.

We got along well. I felt kinda . . . married, but still kinda . . . not.

～

Any actor starting out will, at some point, need to join the Actors' Equity Association (or just Equity), the union for actors appearing on stage. The catch-22 of becoming a member is this: You can't join the union without a job, and you can't get a job without joining the union. There was also the Screen Actors Guild (or just SAG) for work in films and the American Federation of Television and Radio Artists (or just AFTRA), both with the same restrictions. I could not yet join these unions, so I had to seek out low-paying jobs in other places.

In a show business trade paper, I saw an ad:

WANTED

Actors to Perform in Children's Theatre

It turned out to be a mom-and-pop business. The wife adapted stories from classic children's books and expanded them into one-hour stage plays, which she also directed. Her husband built the scenery. The plays would be performed at schools in and around New York. It was a non-Equity company and paid five dollars a performance. That was not a lot of money, but actors would do anything just to practice their craft; they'd even work for free. I met the director and became a part of her traveling cast.

Doing these shows for a few months taught me an important lesson. I learned that our audiences (about seven to ten years old) were at times involved in our plays, but often bored too.

They only really came to life when one actor was "sneaking up" on another actor. For some reason, they loved this. They would gasp, then warn the innocent character of the danger. That was always the highlight of the show.

I learned that the director charged $100 for the plays, so I decided to put together a show of my own. Since I'd played a clown a few times in college, I could juggle a little and I knew some magic tricks, so I'd

Clowning around to pay the rent.

PHOTO BY PETER PERRI

offer schools a forty-five-minute show for $75. One or two shows a month would keep me going. I found my old college clown outfit, and once again I became . . . Dooley the Clown.

I knew I couldn't stretch my clowning for forty-five minutes, so I found another actor and put together a ringmaster's costume for him with a top hat and tails. Together we filled up the time.

To get my clown show started, I wanted to use the "sneaking up" moment that was always so reliable. My partner, Professor Knickerbocker, would enter to tell the kids that the Dooleyville Train had been delayed. The children were disappointed. He began to read them a boring story. The kids were yawning. I was behind the curtain, and, as he droned on, I started to shake the curtain. The kids knew something was up. Somebody (possibly the clown) was "sneaking up" on the professor. They started to laugh. When the professor went to the right to investigate, I went to the left to shake the curtain. Finally, I stuck out my white-gloved hand and waved. Now the kids were really "caught up in the comedy." The professor was like the teacher or the parent. I was the mischievous child, more like them. Then I pushed my big, colorful clown shoe out through the curtain. Big laugh. Then I poked my whole body out all at once. Even bigger laugh. I sometimes stretched this out for four or five minutes.

What I learned from all this helped me to understand how comedy could apply to dramatic structure, plot, suspense, and character development as well. That clown show always came in handy when I needed to pay the rent.

~

I had been in New York now for quite a while. For much of that time I'd have a job in show business, then I'd have a dry spell. I had some pretty good parts but never made quite enough money to get ahead.

Then I got a lucky break. There was a radio show called *Bobby Benson and the B-Bar-B*. Bobby, who was the star, was twelve years old. As you may have guessed, it was a show for kids. There were three regulars in the cast: Bobby himself, a singing cowboy named Tex, and my friend Don Knotts, who played Windy Wales, teller of tall tales.

The show was broadcast Monday through Friday on the Mutual Network. The producers now wanted to expand the show to TV, a half hour every afternoon. Don made a very nice salary for the radio show, but the TV version would be local, just in New York. Don knew it would be a lot more work for a lot less money. He was the most talented member of the cast, and, of course, his bosses wanted him to do the TV show. Don wanted to keep the radio show but not do the TV show.

The day he was to tell them he wanted out of the TV version, and knowing they'd be upset, he concocted a story. He would tell them he already had his replacement; it would be Windy's nephew, a not-too-smart cowboy who could draw cartoons, juggle, and do magic. Guess who that would be?

I had rented a cowboy outfit and a carpetbag full of props. Don had hidden me in an empty office in the building and had me come in to the meeting. We had written a short comedy routine about our family. I did a few tricks, and it worked. He kept the radio job; I got the TV gig.

The show was a great opportunity for me. For just a couple of hours a day I was paid $125 a week. Less than a year in New York, and I was on TV! I finally joined AFTRA. The show lasted only six months, but I was able to put some money in the bank.

I still did not have an agent to represent me; agents get 10 percent of your salary. I was not smart enough to figure out that any agent would sign me as a client for a mere $12.50 commission a week. But I thought, *Hey! I'm already working! I don't need an agent!* It looked like I had a lot to learn. I was still Paul Brown.

13
Off-Broadway

At a small theater in Greenwich Village called Originals Only Playhouse, I landed a part in *One Foot to the Sea*, a drama set aboard a ship (not in the Navy, but in the Merchant Marine) about two men who are in love but dare not let it be known; not at that time, anyway. Until then, there had been only a few plays with that theme, but everything about them had to be hidden. *One Foot* was a very good, very touching drama.

I played a sailor with a Cockney accent. At one moment in the play, I was standing on a kind of dock and the stage was dark, with the fog creeping on stage. Looking at all this, I mumbled, "Look at it! Look at the mucking fog!"

I was always worried that I might transpose the words into something, well . . . sexual. One night, it happened, I said the line the wrong way. But instead of being shocked, the audience laughed. Later, the director was furious, thinking I'd done it on purpose. I explained it was just a mistake and told him the playwright should have known that those two words were an accident waiting to happen. He said, "Oh, okay . . . what the hell is a 'mog' anyway?"

One of the actors in the play was John Astin, who would later star in the TV series *The Addams Family* and many other TV shows and movies.

After a short run, our play was about to close and John Astin got a part in another show, a musical, *The Threepenny Opera*, written by Bertolt Brecht with music by Kurt Weill. *Threepenny* had originally played in Berlin, and this would be the New York debut. Astin recommended me and later I met with the director, Carmine Capalbo, and was hired as one of "Mack-the-Knife's" gang—I was Walt Dreary. The cast would include Beatrice Arthur (later to star in TV's *Maude*, and later still, in *The Golden Girls*), Charlotte Rae (later to star in TV's *The Facts of Life*), and a group of other talented actors and singers.

I went with the costume designer for *Threepenny* to a costume shop on Second Avenue, an area that, for years, had been the center of plays done in Yiddish. We were in a shop trying on clothing from a bygone time. The owner, quite an old man with a thick accent, was one Mr. Gropper.

From his back room he had produced some outfits to be considered: coats, pants, hats. I had tried on pants, which were chosen, a derby from the period, and was now trying on coats. The designer was not only looking at size and fit, but also colors and styles. He had rejected a number of coats when I tried on the last of them, a tailcoat with a checkered pattern. The designer, still not satisfied, said, with the wave of his hand, "No. No. That will never do." Mr. Gropper had had enough. He yelled . . .

"Never do? Vot never do! Jacob Ben-Ami vore dat coat! Boris Thomashefsky vore dat coat!! Menasha Skulnik vore dat coat!!!"

He continued giving the *credits . . . of the coat.* That coat had quite an impressive résumé . . . certainly better than mine. Mr. Gropper had been insulted on *behalf* of that coat.

After rehearsals I began to explore Greenwich Village, where the show would be playing at the Theatre de Lys. "The Village," as it was known, had a Bohemian quality and for years had been home to writers, painters, actors, singers, dancers, sculptors, and musicians. The narrow streets featured art galleries, antiques stores, vintage clothing places, jewelry shops, and restaurants. It was a friendly, creative place to live.

At that time in the Village there were only three theaters that were well known, though still not considered Broadway theaters: the Cherry Lane Theater, the Theatre de Lys, and the Circle in the Square. Circle would emerge as the most successful of the three.

Under the direction of Jose Quintero, a series of plays were so well reviewed they put Circle on the map. One of them was *The Iceman*

Cometh, by Eugene O'Neill. It starred Jason Robards, making him a star, and brought uptown lovers of theater flocking down to the Village in droves. Another early production was *Summer and Smoke*, by Tennessee Williams starring Geraldine Page, making her a star. All this excitement gave birth to the Off-Broadway movement.

I got to thinking . . . *Threepenny is going to be a big deal, maybe this is a good time to change my name.* I had already learned that there was an actor on Broadway named Paul Brown. He was obviously in Actors Equity, and the union wouldn't allow a new member to use the same name. That settled it! I was now . . . Paul Dooley.

I've always had this . . . identity problem. I think a lot of actors do. Why are we happier pretending to be other people rather than ourselves? I think it might come from low self-esteem.

For me, the clues were everywhere. Looking for a nickname, finding a cartoonist name, a clown name, even a stage name. I finally made my name change *legal* so if I ever had children, they could carry on the *fake* family name with pride.

~

Threepenny was a wonderful experience. The cynical story and the dissonant music gave it a very different perspective for a musical. The star was Lotte Lenya, the wife of the composer, Kurt Weill. She had starred in *Threepenny* on the stage in Berlin and, later in the 1930s, in the film based on the musical. She was well-known in Europe and had made recordings of Weill's music. In the original production she had played the part of Pirate Jenny, a prostitute and one of Mack-the-Knife's many lovers. She was perhaps in her twenties then and in her forties now, still playing the same role.

Lenya was a wonderful singer with a throaty, sexy, world-weary voice, and when she sang the song "The Black Freighter," everyone backstage stopped what they were doing and listened. It was always a magical moment.

The show was a big hit. We got rave reviews and were selling out. Well-known producers wanted to move the show to Broadway. They were told, "No! This show belongs in a small theater; it's about whores, beggars, and crooks." We stayed at the Theatre de Lys. I was there for three months and then decided to move on. In the end, the play would last for seven years.

14
He Put Words in My Mouth

An ad in the paper: Gagwriters Workshop. I decided to investigate. I found a big rehearsal room rented by the hour with a basket by the door and a sign: Admission 25¢.

The instructor told us he had worked in Hollywood as a writer for comedians (he mentioned Bob Hope, for one). He seemed to me kind of over-the-hill. I thought, *Why was he teaching comedy writing for twenty-five cents a night?*

There were about thirty people in the room. After a few meetings, I realized I wasn't going to get anything out of this. A few so-called comedians would get up and tell a few so-called jokes. The jokes weren't funny, and neither were the comedians.

Except for one. His name was Fred Willard, and he was extremely funny (as the world would one day discover). Fred, wisely, dropped out of Gagwriter's Workshop. I stayed.

One night, another fellow got up. He seemed uncomfortable. I didn't think he was a performer, maybe he was a writer. He started reading a monologue he had written, and it knocked my socks off. His jokes were unlike anything I'd ever heard. Smarter, more offbeat, actually literary, he was unique, and his writing was brilliant.

> There's a small village in a third world country . . .
> very primitive. They don't actually use money; their
> medium of exchange is the water buffalo . . . Any-
> thing you pay for, you will use a water buffalo. It's a

pretty good system, but they're having a *little trouble*
with the parking meters.

His name was David Panich. He was a schoolteacher and about my
age. I approached him and complimented him, and we became friends.
We soon stopped going to the Gagwriter's Workshop, now that I had
a writer of my own. David was a bit of an oddball, with no real social
skills. He could seem standoffish, but, over time, I learned he was actually just wary of other people. I didn't care about any of that. I was
drawn to his comedy mind. I told David I'd like to work up enough of
an act to make a few dollars as a stand-up comic.

. I couldn't afford to pay him what he was worth but promised that
when I made some money, I'd share it with him. He didn't mind; he just
wanted his humor to be heard.

I could have just let him work alone, picked up his pages, and then
discussed them. I chose, instead, to be with him as he wrote. So, every
Saturday, I'd go to his house on Long Island, where he lived with his
mother.

Here's another sample of David's gift for offbeat comedy:

> My son, who is eight, goes to a very progressive
> school. On parents' day I went there to observe what
> went on. Two boys got into a scuffle. The teacher
> said, "Tommy, stop pulling Michael's ear! Do you
> think you'll prove you're *stronger* by pulling Michael's
> ear? Do you think you'll prove you're *better* by pulling
> Michael's ear? Tommy, come up here to my desk!
> Now . . . give me that ear!"

I would sit with David and watch him create. He'd write down a
joke, show it to me, take it back, cut out a few words (like he was a
surgeon), and make it better.

Being there when a really good joke was being born was thrilling. Our goal was to create, for me, thirty minutes of comedy, but because of his high standards, and many false starts, it took about six months. In the process, I had been given a master class in comedy.

The act would consist of a Shakespearean play where I played all the parts, a Kurdish fairy tale poorly translated, and a bit of humor about the subway.

> So I'm on the subway, it was rush hour, people
> packed in like sardines, and I happened to notice
> a little old lady near me, and I felt very bad to be
> sitting down, especially
> . . . on her.
> So I said to the guy
> . . . on me:
> Why don't you get up so this little old lady can get
> up?
> I can't, I'm holding another lady's packages.
> Why don't you give them back?
> She's sitting on them.
> Why don't we all get up?
> And so we did, which finally allowed the little old
> lady to get up
> . . . off the little old man
> . . . sitting on the kid
> . . . with the dog.

I would also be performing some of David's beatnik poetry.

> A man who was deeply in debt
> claimed life could be unkind
> he cried, how bad can things get?

and went blind.
and had to beg
until his leg
was broke
and he got a crack
in his head
from a stroke
and bled
and began to choke
causing harm
to his back
and broke his arm
in an attack
of fits
from the gout
and lost his wits
. . . so watch out!!

~

Armed with my "new act," I wanted to try it out and went to an amateur contest in Brooklyn where performers competed for cash prizes.
I was allowed just five minutes. First prize was $10, and second prize
was $5. I won second prize. An agent came backstage and said, "You're
not an amateur, forget about this stuff." He mentioned a cabaret in
Greenwich Village called Upstairs at the Duplex. "You won't get paid,
but you'll fit in there."

He was right about that. The woman who hosted it liked me and
told me I could come back as often as I liked. The room was small but
usually filled with a really smart crowd. The other performers were very
talented and, like me, just beginning their careers. Actor George Segal

(later a movie star) played the banjo and sang. There was also Woody Allen, Joan Rivers, and a lot of others.

Upstairs at the Duplex allowed me to record my complete act with a friendly audience. It became an album released by Strand Records, and, except for the $300 they paid me for the taping, I never made a dime from it. I called it *Paul Dooley: Booked Solid*, hoping that would come true. They gave me a dozen albums for free. I still have four of them . . . (but nothing to play them on).

15
Second Banana

David Panich had gotten a job at a summer resort in Upstate New York and recommended me as a comic. Green Mansions had been there for many years. The guests (most of them returned year after year) were left-leaning socialist types.

When I got there, I found that comedian Bernie West was the star and had spent many summers there. He was the "top banana" (a term used in burlesque to describe the leading comedian). The "second banana" would be a young woman from California named . . . Carol Burnett, and I was just part of the bunch.

The pay was modest, but we lived on a beautiful lake and were given very nice living quarters and three meals a day. During the first week of rehearsals, all the performers were whispering about Carol, "That girl is going to be a star!" She was in her early twenties, and it was clear, even at this young age, that Carol was a gifted comic actress.

We did comedy sketches together all summer. I'll never forget how much fun it was working with her.

Green Mansions was known for its entertainment, and there was a lot of it; the guests got their money's worth. There would be a play on Monday evening, a string quartet on Tuesday, a musical on Wednesday, opera singers on Thursday, an evening of poetry on Friday, and on Saturday an original revue of songs, dances, and sketches created by staff writers, lyricists, and composers who lived on the grounds. Our resident lyricist was Sheldon Harnick, fresh out of Northwestern University, who later was one of the creators of the legendary musical *Fiddler on the Roof*.

Sunday evening there was a variety show. Anyone who had an act of any kind could join in. There was a dance team, Bernie and I did monologues, and Carol sang funny songs. It was a very creative place to spend the summer.

There was a director, a choreographer, a conductor and a large orchestra, half a dozen dancers, several singers, and two or three opera singers, and everyone was to double as actors in all the plays and musicals.

Oddly, one of the shows we did was *The Threepenny Opera*, which I had just left in New York. Carol was now playing the Lotte Lenya role, the prostitute "Pirate Jenny."

The real bonus for the performers and writers was that, on Labor Day weekend, all the top agents from New York came to see a "best of" show with the highlights of the season. They were looking for talent for upcoming Broadway plays and musicals and even TV shows.

Possibly because I had spent the summer at Green Mansions, I got to know a lot of people from the world of revue. A revue is not a play or a musical. To begin with, there is no story and no plot, just a collection of comedy sketches and songs, not unlike *Saturday Night Live*. But instead of being on TV, a revue would normally be in a theater, a nightclub, or a cabaret.

16
Timberland

A friend of mine, Bobby Kessler, reached out to me and asked if I'd like to join him and his partner, Martin Charnin, to do shows at a summer resort called Timberland. Bobby and Marty were songwriters, and I was to be the leading comedian in the company. The camp was located in Upstate New York not far from Green Mansions.

Timberland was not nearly as big or as popular as Mansions, so our shows were a low-budget version of theirs. In contrast with the large orchestra at Mansions, we had a trio. Mansions had more than twenty performers; at Timberland we had five.

That summer was hectic but also very exciting. There was a young woman in the company, I'll call her Sarah (not her real name). Sarah had talent; she could act, she could sing, and everybody liked her. She had a charming smile, and I thought she was very cute.

I asked her, "Where's your hometown?" "Oshkosh," she said. I liked that name. I liked her. There seemed to be a mutual attraction, and over the summer we became involved.

Often a summer romance will end at the end of summer, but when Sarah and I returned to Manhattan, we continued our relationship. Sarah was quite serious about it. She knew what she wanted, and she wanted me to get a divorce. In fact, she wanted to get married. *Married?* I thought, *I'm already married.* I wasn't sure what to do. So, foolishly I did nothing and we kept seeing each other.

~

Loretta and I had been living together for several years as man and wife. I felt it was time to tell her about Sarah. We both knew, with her travel and my out-of-town jobs, something like this might be inevitable. Although I felt very close to her and we had a history together, our relationship had been a "marriage of convenience." We agreed to a divorce, and Sarah and I got married. It was a simple ceremony with just a few friends attending.

We had very little money coming in. My clown bookings had slowed down, and I was on unemployment. Sarah did temp jobs as a secretary. We found an affordable apartment in the Chelsea neighborhood. Our budget allowed little for anything but rent and meals. There was a lot of Campbell's soup: chicken noodle, vegetable beef, and mushroom; also tuna salad and baked beans . . . nothing fancy. But—we were somehow getting by.

~

My mother was fond of Loretta and had gotten to know her on visits to New York. I knew she wouldn't like me divorcing Loretta and right away marrying someone she'd never heard of. I put off telling my mother about it. Sarah kept asking, "Did you tell your mother we're married?" I'd say, "Not yet, but I will." After a couple of months, she took matters into her own hands and wrote my mother, telling her everything. My mother was upset and so was Sarah. They had started out on the wrong foot. I blamed myself. I didn't handle that situation well at all.

After my mother had time to reconsider, she decided to send Sarah a belated wedding gift. At that time there was a skin product to help women with blemishes, acne, and the like, and it was called Vanishing Cream. That choice for a wedding gift, I thought, spoke volumes. Freud would have loved it.

~

I'd been keeping track of Carol Burnett. She had been booked into The Blue Angel, a swank Manhattan supper club, and she needed a new song. Carol's vocal coach, Ken Welch, had an idea. "What if you're this young girl, and instead of going crazy for Elvis, she has the hots for an older boring guy?" He wrote the song "I Made a Fool of Myself over John Foster Dulles." Dulles was Eisenhower's secretary of state and hardly someone a young girl might fall for. She sang the song at the club, and it became the *talk of the town*. She was asked to sing it on Jack Paar's *Tonight Show*.

As Carol tells the story, "I sang the song on Tuesday. The next day, someone from Washington called to say that Mr. Dulles had missed it and could I go back on the show and sing it again. So, on Thursday, I sang it again. I was then invited to appear on *The Ed Sullivan Show* on Sunday to sing it one more time." That appearance had created a sensation and now a nationwide audience had discovered Carol Burnett; she was twenty-four years old.

Next, she joined *The Garry Moore Show*, a TV variety show that had been on CBS for several years. Garry Moore was a very charming, well-liked performer, but Carol was such a powerful comic talent that she soon became the de facto star. Carol recommended me from time to time when the show needed an extra actor.

With a summer off from TV, Carol went to another resort. Just like Mansions, Camp Tamiment was equally famous and also known for its original revues. I'm sure Carol was a great success there. One of the most famous performers to come out of Tamiment directly to TV was comedian Sid Caesar.

Tamiment also had agents, producers, and directors show up on Labor Day weekend to look for talent. A number of these revues and musicals ended up on Broadway. Carol made her Broadway debut starring in *Once Upon a Mattress* and took New York by storm.

When the *Garry Moore Show* ended, CBS was anxious to give Carol her own show. Carol wasn't sure she wanted that, telling them she didn't want the responsibility of an entire show on her shoulders and that she would much prefer to be one of a group putting on a show. CBS gave her what she wanted. The program was called *The Entertainers*. The stars were Carol, comedian Bob Newhart, singer Caterina Valente, comic Dom DeLuise, and singer John Davidson. Because Carol and I were friends, I was also a guest on some of those shows. *The Entertainers* lasted for one season, and then Carol told CBS, "Okay, I'll do my own show." The new one, now called *The Carol Burnett Show*, ran for eleven years and finally made Carol the star she was always meant to be.

~

My friend David Panich had been one of the writers on *The Entertainers*, along with another writer, a young woman named Treva Silverman. When that show ended after a year, the two of them headed for Los Angeles (LA). David worked on a number of shows and ended up on *Laugh In*, a very popular TV show at the time.

Treva, who was a very talented comedy writer, first worked on *The Monkees*. She wrote for other shows as well, finally joining *The Mary Tyler Moore Show* in the early years. She had perfect pitch writing for Valerie Harper, who played Mary's neighbor Rhoda, and in one year she won, not one, but two Emmy Awards. She and I are still friends.

17
The Vanguard

The Village Vanguard is a famous Greenwich Village nightclub. It started out in the 1930s and originally featured folk music. Later it became a jazz club. I knew it only from the 1950s. At that time, it featured such jazz legends as Charlie Parker, Miles Davis, John Coltrane, and Dizzy Gillespie, to name a few.

I worked there for about six months (another part-time job paying five bucks a night), first as a car parker, then as a doorman, and finally as a maître d' (which is a fancy name for someone who shows you to your table). In that capacity I was in the room where all these amazing jazz musicians performed.

The owners of the Vanguard were particular about what comics worked there. They only booked those whose style fit in with jazz. They were usually very hip, very smart, and improvisational, just like the jazz men.

A friend said to me, "You mean you get to see Miles Davis and Charlie Parker for free?" I'd say, "Better yet, I get to see Lenny Bruce, Mort Sahl, and Professor Irwin Corey for free." These comics were very hot at that time, and I was such a fan (and such a sponge) that over time I memorized their acts.

Especially exciting was Lenny Bruce, who was just breaking out as the most important comedian in the country. He was outrageous. They called him a "sick" comic. He said things and did things that no one else had ever said or done. He made fun of the Vatican, the Pope, and even the police. He was regularly arrested and taken to court; he always went after the Establishment.

He was, however, not just trying to shock his audience. He had something to say about our culture, our hypocrisy . . . and especially, our prejudices. He was a crusader, and nearly every comedian who came after him was influenced by Lenny Bruce. Mort Sahl came onstage carrying a newspaper. He had a collegiate quality and did mostly political humor. There was also Professor Irwin Corey, the World's Foremost Authority, who I felt was hilarious. More about him later.

One night, the comedy team of Mike Nichols and Elaine May came to the Vanguard; their first time in New York. Those two had gotten their start at Chicago's Compass Players, then left that group to go out on their own. Their act was a collection of scenes born out of improvisation and was totally original. There were no jokes, just behavior and attitudes satirizing characters from life.

They were amazing. So clever, so witty, so fresh. In no time they were booked into The Blue Angel. They next appeared on Jack Paar's *Tonight Show.* They were on NBC Radio. They soon became the darlings of New York's high society. Not long after that they did their own Broadway show.

Mike and Elaine stopped working as a team and went on to have separate careers. Elaine worked as a writer, a director, and an actress for film and the stage. She was often hired as a "script doctor" in Hollywood to fix ailing screenplays . . . a very lucrative day job.

Mike became a director on Broadway. In fact, he became *the* most successful stage director in New York. In a period of eighteen months, he directed *Barefoot in the Park*, *The Odd Couple*, *Luv*, and *The Knack* and won the Tony Award three times in a row. He then directed the film *Who's Afraid of Virginia Woolf* with Elizabeth Taylor and Richard

Mike Nichols and Elaine May. Brilliant! PBS/PHOTOFEST ©PBS

Burton and won his first Oscar for directing *The Graduate* with Dustin
Hoffman and Anne Bancroft and continued a distinguished career for
years in Hollywood. His biggest triumph, I believe, was for directing
Angels in America on television. Mike was an EGOT (which stands for
a winner of the Emmy, Grammy, Oscar, and Tony Awards).

Mike and Elaine reunited later for the films *Primary Colors* and *The
Birdcage.*

In time, I was privileged to work with both of them.

~

Acting jobs were few and far between, but I had landed some small parts
on TV shows, such as *The Defenders*; *East Side/West Side*, with George
C. Scott and Cicely Tyson; and *Bilko*, with the great Phil Silvers.

18
Stand Up and Be Counted

I got a booking to do my stand-up act in the little village of Upper Saddle River, New Jersey. The audience would be a group of CPAs and their wives. I didn't know what to expect, but they were very receptive. I did my thirty minutes; they laughed a lot, and I picked up my $25 and headed home.

A few days later I got a call from a man named George Spota, a manager who represented comedians, among others. In his office the next day, he explained that his brother-in-law was a CPA who had seen me do my act the past weekend and thought I was very funny and had a fresh new style. I then performed some of my material for him, an audience of one. He was friendly but didn't laugh much. Two days later he told me I had an audition for *The Tonight Show*. I was dumbfounded. At that point I'd only had, maybe, a dozen bookings and was still learning how to do stand-up. I felt I wasn't ready. Successful comics, with years of experience, were trying to do that show. To make an appearance there would be a huge stepping-stone for me . . . but I had to be good enough.

The *Tonight Show* was extremely popular. The first host was Steve Allen, who was there for several years. Now the star of the show was a fellow named Jack Paar.

I wondered how this manager had so much influence at the show. It turned out, his star client was the genius Jonathan Winters, who was Jack Paar's favorite and had done the show dozens of times.

At my audition I met Jack Paar and some of his staff. We all said hello and I began. My act was a little unusual in that a typical comedian would tell a series of short jokes on a subject and then move on to another subject. My act was thirty minutes of longer scenes, each with a beginning, middle, and end, more like one-act plays.

I began with my Shakespeare routine. Since my act sometimes needed a little music here and there, Sarah came along to play the piano for me. They smiled nicely and said, "What else do you have?" I ran through my whole act and got, "What else do you have?" over and over. I was finished. The next time they said, "What else?" I was stuck. Then I remembered something David and I had worked on but hadn't finished. It was a way-out-there idea about a five-year-old boy as president of the United States. I ad-libbed my way through two or three minutes. They laughed and said, "That's funny! Can you do the show next week?"

David and I quickly finished the routine. I now had my six minutes. Jack Paar gave me a nice introduction. I was very nervous. I had never done this routine before an audience. I would be flying blind. It started slow, but finally I was getting laughs. It ended well, and Paar said a few kind words and also said he'd be inviting me back. Sitting on his couch that night were Sammy Davis Jr. and the great comedy team of Bob and Ray. At that time *The Tonight Show* paid about $350 to guests; I gave David Panich half the money.

I have a recording of that first appearance, and it's painful for me to watch. I can see how nervous I was and how insecure; I hadn't yet perfected that routine. The jokes were very good, so I got laughs, but I wish it had gone smoother. Still . . . it kicked off my career as a comedian.

The Tonight Show producers contacted me and asked if I was available to do the show again in two weeks. I told them, "Yes," even though I had no new material. At the audition they had not shown much interest in any of my regular routines, and now I was out on a limb. My friend David had written the lion's share of everything I did, but he was still teaching school and unavailable. Now what was I going to do?

By chance I ran into Alan Alda, whom I had met once before. I knew he was an actor but had heard he was also a writer. His father, Robert Alda, had starred on Broadway in *Guys and Dolls*. Alan told me his dad had also worked in burlesque as a singer and straight man, and Alan had grown up backstage listening to burlesque comedy. I asked him if he could help me write a routine for *The Tonight Show*, and he said he'd be happy to.

We began meeting, but we needed an idea or a premise to start with. We saw a photo on the front page of the *New York Post*: Mayor Wagner had been visiting a school, trailed by reporters. In a hallway, a large rat ran across his path. The cameras caught a picture of the rat . . . and the mayor's reaction.

We laughed and realized this could be our premise, a run-down school with an underpaid teacher. In no time, we put together the routine. It went very well with the live audience on *The Tonight Show*. I was happy. I gave half my money to Alan. He was happy too.

～

Remembering Alan reminds me of how we first met. It had to have been in the 1950s. As a clown, I had worked, sometimes, for a company that provided performers for special events like grand openings of a supermarket or a pizzeria. I would show up in my clown costume and work on the street to draw attention to the store, sometimes handing out coupons or cheap gifts.

Irv West, my ringmaster partner, called to ask a favor. He knew a young actor with a wife and two kids who needed work. He wanted to help him get some special event jobs and asked me, "Could you loan him a clown outfit?" I said, "Sure. Send him over to my place."

He turned out to be Alan Alda.

I gave him a colorful, one-piece jumpsuit with a long zipper. I then gave him a funny hat, a red rubber ball for a nose, and some clown white makeup. He did these jobs for a while, and then I lost track of him.

By the way, in my sixty-five years as an actor, I've met hundreds of actors, writers, directors, all very nice people . . . but none of them as nice as Alan Alda. He is very open, very kind, very caring. He's generous and extremely compassionate. It's impossible not to like him.

The Tonight Show opened doors for me. The agent started booking me all over, including the Playboy Club in Chicago (I went to the Playboy mansion and met Hugh Hefner). I played a club in Dallas, and when I got back to New York, I appeared at the Show Place, the Living Room, and a club called the Bon Soir, where the crowd was great. That's where I first met Barbra Streisand, who was playing the same club. She was quite young at the time but with a real stage presence, and what a voice! I learned that we had the same manager. His clients were Barbra, David Panich, and myself. The manager turned out to be a crook who cheated us on our earnings. We all fired him.

~

My four weeks in Chicago were cut down to two, and my two weeks in Dallas ended in one. I was told by my agent that my act wasn't "commercial" enough, that the audience didn't get my humor out of town. He felt it was too "inside," too "clever" for them. However, I loved working in New York and I always did well there. But I was tired of being canceled and lonely in my hotel rooms. I decided to give up stand-up . . . at least "on the road."

~

I heard from the folks at Camp Tamiment that they wanted me to join them for the summer. I would be the leading comic, now the "top banana." Sarah came for a visit while I was there.

That's where I met Pat McCormick. The outrageous and very funny comedy writer would later write jokes for *The Tonight Show*, especially with Johnny Carson, for many, many years and would become a legend as a comedy writer. We shared a room that summer.

I also got to know Bob Ross. He was on the social director staff. His job was to keep the guests from being bored. When a group of them were gathered, he would find ways to entertain them. Often, he was referred to as the "pool comic" . . . or if it was raining, the "porch comic." His job required him to do anything for a laugh.

Bob also appeared on our main stage when another actor was needed. Bob went on to do a lot of TV as well as theater. He was a very funny guy, always very upbeat, and he also loved vaudeville. We've been friends for sixty years.

~

Here are some "Great Moments in Comedy" (at least for me).

The shortest sentence (just four words), and the funniest one ever, in any movie, was in *Young Frankenstein*. Those words were spoken (sort of) by Peter Boyle as the Monster, as he tried, gamely, to sing along with Gene Wilder's Doctor, in his demented attempt at musical comedy. You guessed it, it was . . .

"Puttin' on the Ritz"!

Orson Bean, a fresh-faced, likeable storyteller, was a comedian I enjoyed. His opening line was, "My name is Orson Bean . . . Harvard '52 . . . Yale nothing."

There was a moment in his act when he was looking at a newspaper and reading his version of "Letters to the Editor." He'd read a letter asking advice signed just with the person's initials and then have a comic answer. There were three letters signed: Mrs. M. B. Chicago, Mr. J. K. Boston, Mrs. L. F. New York New York . . . New York. He had added an extra New York.

Then, *unbelievably*, he *tipped* the newspaper forward and *shook it gently to get rid of the extra New York*. That idea was so subtle, yet so funny, it really impressed me.

Professor Irwin Corey, the World's Foremost Authority, was unique. He wore a tailcoat, dark baggy pants, a string tie, and ratty-looking white sneakers. He played the role of a demented professor; the audience was his class. Corey was famous for his opening. He spent four or five minutes trying to get started with his remarks, all in silence. When he finally spoke, he said, "However—"

In 1960, people were raving about an Off-Broadway sketch show called *Stewed Prunes*, starring Richard Libertini and MacIntyre Dixon. These two proved to be "comedy gold"; part vaudeville, part pantomime, part genius, and totally original. I'll describe just one wonderful scene.

Libertini enters to introduce the first contestant in an animal talent show . . . but without words. "Woof woof," he says, "woof woof woof" with the cadence and emphasis that tell us exactly what he means. Enter Dixon as a cat singing a lovely ballad . . . "Meow meow . . . meow meow meow." He smiles, bows, and exits.

Libertini enters, thanks him, and introduces the next act, "Woof woof woof," and so on. Dixon comes onstage with an orange wig and, as a lion, he roars a dramatic speech from Shakespeare, "Rahr rahr . . . rahr rahr rahr" . . . and exits.

Libertini comes on, woof-woofing the next act. Surprise! Surprise! It's Dixon, as a goat who does impressions. He bleats an introduction. "Mmeh mmeh . . . mmeh," and then says, "Mooo," smiles, and bows. He then begins his next impression saying, "Woof woof . . . woof."

Libertini, annoyed, leans out from the wings, chastising him and woofing a warning ("Hey! Knock it off!"). Dixon, as the goat, bleats an apology and then goes into his last impression . . . his big finish. He turns his back to the audience, rearranges his hair, turns back and says, "Down Boy!" I thought, *What a great idea! A goat impersonating a human!*

To me, those inspired moments of humor made all those performers . . . "Unsung Heroes of Comedy!"

19
Fabulous

I would audition often for TV commercials. I had an agent who thought I'd be good at it. She would submit me all the time, but I would never get the job.

After failing, maybe ten times, at a commercial audition, I'd think, *This is something I just can't do.* Then, after another twenty auditions, I lost even more confidence. Each time I tried and failed, I'm sure I did my auditions in a defeated way, which would, of course . . . defeat me.

I know I had done at least forty of these auditions when one came along that would change everything. It was 1961, and the agent called, excited, saying, "You got it!" The product was a laundry detergent called Fab. I would be playing a likeable, but bumbling, door-to-door sales-man. The client ("Mr. Fab" . . . I guess) loved the commercial, loved me, and wanted to put me under contract as their spokesman. I could hardly believe it.

After getting by for nine years on $3,000 a year (and sometimes less), the new contract guaranteed me $40,000 a year; that's more than $300,000 in today's dollars. It was like winning the lottery. I finally joined the Screen Actors Guild.

I did a lot of commercials for Fab. These TV spots played constantly, and since Fab was a soap, our audience would be housewives. It was on TV many times a day on all the networks.

As the "Fab" Salesman. AUTHOR'S COLLECTION.

That's when I learned the most beautiful word in the English language . . . residuals.

~

Sarah and I took a belated honeymoon to Jamaica, where we spent a stress-free week. It's a beautiful place and we enjoyed it a lot. To my surprise, when we returned home, Sarah suggested therapy. And to my further surprise, I realized it was a good idea. So . . . we went to see an analyst. He said he'd be happy to help but would work only with one of us. He recommended another therapist for me; his name was Dan Kaplowitz. I liked him, and I spent months working with him. My wife, on the other hand, soon grew dissatisfied with her therapist and a short time later left him. She didn't say why, but since I felt I was learning something about myself, I continued with Dr. K.

~

In the early 1960s Sarah was expecting, and Robin, dear, sweet Robin, came into our lives that year. She was born in December, but to us she was like the "first robin of spring."

Robin's arrival was life-changing. I loved her, loved being a dad, especially with the security of money in the bank. I felt more centered, more involved, thinking less about work and more about family. Having a child had certainly brought my wife and me closer.

Baby Robin. She was like the "first robin of spring."
AUTHOR'S COLLECTION.

20
Brooklyn

Sarah started looking for a new home. She found one in the Cobble Hill section of Brooklyn, and it was, indeed, a find. There were three stories and six rooms, in an off-the-main-street row of thirteen brick houses facing thirteen others with a shared garden between them. All of this was surrounded by iron gates, front and back, and only homeowners had keys. Perfect for families with children. The complex had been designed by a famous architect and had been designated a landmark. I paid only $14,900 for the house . . . with a mortgage, of course.

We were happy there. After living in apartments for so many years, it was great for me to have a real home and a new child (Robin was about one now). At that time there were a number of books about the best ways to raise children, especially those by well-known pediatrician Dr. Benjamin Spock. Sarah read them all. I was impressed with what she was learning, and she would certainly be a very good mother.

With Robin I was a hands-on dad. I changed my share of diapers, gave her baths, took her for trips to a nearby park, and read her bedtime stories. I remember *Winnie the Pooh* and *The Cat in the Hat*, and she never tired of *Goodnight Moon*, *Pierre*, and *In the Night Kitchen*. Those last two, by artist Maurice Sendak, I also enjoyed a lot. Fatherhood was a lot of fun.

Those early 1960s were good years for us. Thanks to "Fab" we furnished our new home and bought a station wagon. We went on trips, visited Sarah's folks in the Midwest, and didn't have to worry about what we were spending.

Because Sarah played, we bought an upright piano. The day it arrived, the deliverymen found they couldn't bring it up the winding staircase.

Instead, they took it back outside, rigged up pulleys and ropes, and pulled it up and in through a very large window in the master bedroom.

~

Once, in Brooklyn, my love of jokes almost got me arrested. I could now park my car on the street, but every other day I had to move it so I wouldn't get a ticket.

One morning I woke up late; it was five minutes to ten. I had to move the car. So, I jumped out of bed, put on a pair of cut-off jeans, and ran out the door. No shirt, no shoes, didn't even take my wallet. It was summer. It was only gonna take me two minutes, but there were no parking spaces across the street. I decided to go around the corner. At the first red light I stopped short. I was in a crosswalk. A cop came over.

"You can't park here."

"Look, I'll just back up. I live right around the corner. I'm just moving my car so I won't get a ticket."

"You're still gonna get a ticket, you're parked in the crosswalk . . . do you have a license?"

I guess I looked like I didn't, in fact, I looked naked.

"Yeah, but I just ran out to move my car . . . I left it at home."

"You got a registration?"

"Again . . . I left it at home."

He took a step back and said:

"Do you have a *gun?*"

"Yeah, but I left it at home."

Now he looked like he was gonna call for backup.

"I'm sorry, Officer. I don't have a gun. I'm an actor. I love jokes. You just gave me the perfect setup."

"Oh, you're an actor, huh?"

I happened to have some pictures in the front seat.

"Yeah—look, here's a picture of me. And on the back is a list of all the shows I've done."

He looked at my résumé . . .

"You were in *Twelve Angry Men*? I saw that show, which one were you?"

"Uh . . . number eleven." (*I lied.*) "One of the least angry men."

"Alright! Get outta here! Go home and get dressed!"

He kept the picture.

~

One Christmas, using her sewing machine, Sarah had created matching polka-dot mother and daughter bathrobes for Robin and herself. I loved how creative she had been in doing this. She was quite resourceful; we once found an adorable kid-sized easy chair at a yard sale. Sarah brought it home, took it apart, and reupholstered it with a pretty fabric. How she did all that I have no idea, but it made a charming gift for our daughter.

Sarah was very thoughtful when giving gifts, always finding the perfect present for Robin and me, as well as for friends. At Christmas, she would always make a sort of holiday treat combining three different types of cereal and trail mix. She'd warm it in the oven with spices, place it in jars with a red ribbon, and give the jars to neighbors, but she would always save some for us as well.

One day, Sarah said to Robin, "Oh, Daddy's on TV." It was a commercial. Robin ran to get her step stool in the bathroom, the one she used to brush her teeth, and also to watch TV . . . when she got back the commercial was over.

On another occasion, Robin was watching TV and my friend Andrew Duncan was on a commercial for Oscar Mayer Wieners. My wife told her, "That's Daddy's friend." Later, when Robin was talking to another kid, she said, "My daddy's friend is the Oscar Mayer Wiener."

~

Later, we were looking for a summerhouse, a weekend place. We found one in Putnam Valley, New York. It was a big old Colonial with three bedrooms, nearly two hundred years old. It was kinda run-down, but with five acres, four of them just woods, the property reminded me of my childhood home.

I made an offer and bought the place. I learned later that my wife was disappointed. She had hoped for a cottage by a lake with lots of neighbors, reminding her of *her* childhood summers, but at the time she seemed to go along with my choice. I realized then that we really didn't know how to talk to each other.

21
Having Fun with Commercials

When my Fab contract ended, I was in good shape financially, but my agent told me that I might be "overexposed." In other words, so identified with Fab that other sponsors might not be likely to use me.

As it turned out, the opposite was true. After a whole year with my face on TV, several times a day, I was more well-known than before. I began to do more and more commercials.

About a year later, a friend said to me, "I see you on TV commercials all the time. I can't even get an audition. What's your secret?" I, frankly, didn't have an answer. He was a good actor and extremely funny. He was Italian and kinda looked Italian. As we talked about it, we realized that nearly every actor in TV commercials was white . . . white, white, white. The same thing was pretty much going on with TV programs, like *Leave It to Beaver* and *Father Knows Best*.

However, about that time, due to the civil rights movement, the culture was changing. Madison Avenue realized that they wanted to appeal to a larger audience and considered: maybe we should use some people of color in our commercials. That opened the door for all kinds of ethnic performers; diversity in advertising had arrived, but it would be a long time before real equality was reached.

~

I thought the guys from the ad agencies took making commercials too seriously; they often seemed to be afraid of making some mistake that might upset the "client" and possibly getting fired. Personally, I wasn't worried about what the client thought . . . but I did like to have fun while filming commercials.

Once, while making one for a disposable razor, Gillette Trac-II, I played a guy in his bathroom with a stubble beard about to shave, when magically, another guy pops up in his bathroom promoting a better razor . . . Gillette Trac-II. I say, "Well your razor sounds great! I'll give it a try." The next scene would find me after the shave and looking terrific.

The director handed me a fresh razor, a can of shaving cream, and said, "Go in the bathroom and shave . . . take your time . . . make sure you get a nice clean shave."

In the bathroom I finished my shave, looked in the mirror and thought, *This looks perfect! Wouldn't it be funny if I went back out there with a tiny piece of toilet paper on my chin* (which usually means you have a small cut or a nick).

I stuck the paper on my chin. Then I thought, *No, this won't work, they'll all think I really cut myself and it won't be funny.* I added three more pieces of paper, then four, then five, scattered randomly about my face. *Well now they're going to know it's a joke. This is going to be . . . . so funny!* I added a finishing touch by placing a tiny piece of toilet paper on the end of my nose and left the bathroom.

When the director, the cameraman, the crew, and especially the client (Mr. Gillette Trac-II) saw me, a hush fell over the room. I waited. Not a single person laughed, not even a snicker.

How could they have thought I had accidentally cut my nose? We finished the commercial. I was lucky I wasn't fired . . . but I still think it was hilarious.

My next job would be filming three commercials for M&M's. ("Melts in your Mouth, not in your Hand.") The idea was that I'd be found in very stressful situations and holding a handful of M&M's, parachuting from a plane, riding a bucking-bronco at a rodeo, and shot out of a cannon at the circus (a stuntman actually did all the hard parts,

I just did the talking). The director of these commercials was Michael Cimino, later to win an Oscar for the film *The Deer Hunter*.

For the cannon commercial they needed a shot of me flying through the air. To get this, they outfitted me with hidden wires and pulled me about twenty feet above the studio floor.

I was assured it was perfectly safe, but it didn't *feel* safe. I was, frankly, kind of worried. Once in place and ready to begin the action, there was a delay (there are often delays when filming).

Here I was, high in the air, hanging by wires, not vertically, but hanging horizontally while the crew below was screwing around with something. A minute goes by, then two, and finally three. I'm uncomfortable and I'm getting pissed off. The one thing you never ever do is to say something negative about the product; the client is right there listening. I was holding in my hand a few M&M's. I opened my hand to look at them and I finally yelled very loudly:

"Son of a Bitch! They Melt in Your Hand!"

Another product was for Swanson TV Chicken Dinners. This would not be a commercial but an "industrial film" to entertain everyone back at the home office. The producers were a couple of guys with a good sense of humor. They told me they wanted big laughs. They said I could take the comedy as far as I wanted . . . so I did.

At that time there was a Sunday morning TV show, *The Wide World of Sports*, featuring interviews with athletes who had just won a big game or a trophy. There was a segment called "Up Close and Personal," hosted by sportscaster Jim McKay. I wanted to kid that by following their format but interviewing a chicken.

When making a film of any kind, if there's an animal, a bird, a snake, or even a rat in it, there's always an expert who can help you. We hired a "chicken wrangler" who could get a chicken to play along . . . or appear to.

The chicken and I would be seated in director's chairs. Behind us was a banner reading "Wide World of Chickens." I asked the cameraman to get a two-shot of the chicken and me, then a close-up of me asking questions, then the chicken's close-up for the response. That might call for the chicken to be looking left, looking right, just random movements we could use to make it seem like the stupid chicken was listening and answering. I was holding a mike, which I occasionally inserted into the chicken's close-up.

I was allowed to sit in with the editor, something not usually done. I found an actress, Lynne Lipton, to do a quirky voice for the chicken. Here's an excerpt:

"Good morning. You're on *Up Close and Personal*. Our guest today is Henrietta."

"Oh, just call me Henny."

"Okay. You've had quite a season, Henny."

"It's been okay."

"C'mon, you're being considered for the Hall of Fame."

"I dunno, I'd be happy with the Hall of Hens."

"I'm sure our listeners would like to know how you prepare for a big game?"

"Well, first I meditate."

"I see."

"Although I'm having a little trouble crossing my legs."

"One final question. Where do you see yourself, say . . . a year from now?"

"Oh, I don't know . . . on a fork?"

22
Listen and Agree

For some time, I'd been hearing about this comedy troupe in Chicago—they'd been described as the "smartest, most talented satirists in America." The group was The Second City. Director Paul Sills had nurtured that original company of actors, and together they had turned the act of improvisation into, quite frankly, a "new art form."

Now they were coming to Broadway. I went to see them three times. They were all wonderful. So witty, so original. The show consisted of the best scenes from Chicago. Oddly enough, even with good reviews, Broadway just didn't "get it." It only ran for three months. The show's producers wanted to move the show to Greenwich Village where they had found a cabaret, a less formal space than the Broadway stage. The actors didn't want to make the move; they wanted to go back to Chicago. They complained that they had been working three years without any time off. The producers told them if they would just open the show in the Village, they would get understudies for them and they could all take vacations. They agreed, and the show reopened at Square East in Greenwich Village. It "caught on" with students from New York University, who made it popular. By coincidence, my friend Bobby Kessler had an evening job as the general manager at Square East. He told me the new show was looking for understudies. He said, "The auditions are on Monday, but if you come to the club Sunday evening you can meet the director before anyone else."

I showed up on Sunday and met the director, Larry Arrick, who explained that they needed understudies for all the male actors. I told him I had done stand-up and sketch comedy.

I said, "Would you like me to audition?" He told me, "Yeah," and I asked him, "Where's the script?" "Oh, there's no script," he said.

"The actors have it all in their heads. You can just go on tonight and improvise."

I thought, *Improvise? I've never gone onstage without knowing my lines, and these people are the masters of it.* Still, I knew this was a great opportunity. After their main show they would take suggestions from the audience and then do an open-ended set of improvs. That's when I would join them. I did a scene applying for a job. To give myself a little help, I played an Italian immigrant with a dialect. The scene got laughs, and I was hired.

Each of the four actors took two weeks off. Instead of hiring four understudies, I filled in for all of them. When the actors returned, the producers said, "Well, now you know everything, you might as well stay." So, I became a full member of the company and learned improvisation as I went along.

Soon after I joined the company, Paul Sills came to New York to see how things were going. Paul, of course, was the master of the improvisation movement who'd learned the concept of theater games from his mother, the teacher Viola Spolin. He was the prime mover in Chicago of Playwright's Theatre, the Compass Players, and Second City, and the creator of *Story Theatre* on Broadway.

He decided to hold some workshops with the cast of the show, sort of a refresher course. I had already learned that the first rule of improv was "listen and agree," meaning you should never negate anything your scene partner says; always "Yes, and. . . ." Never "No, but . . ."

In these workshops I learned that a secondary part of any scene might also attempt to "heighten and transform." I was asked to come onstage and do a scene with Barbara Harris, and our audience was the cast of the current show. Paul Sills asked them, "Who are these people?" Someone offered, "Uh, a young married couple." "Where are they?" "Looking for a new home."

As we started improvising, Barbara and I created a house that was a fixer-upper; run-down, old furniture, cobwebs everywhere. Our comments added an old rocking chair, a rolltop desk, and a spinning wheel. There was nothing there, we were just making it up.

We decided to go up an invisible staircase to the attic, where we found a lot of junk, old trunks, and also a dollhouse. I went closer and pretended to open an invisible door, ducked down and went "into" the dollhouse. Barbara followed, then the dollhouse grew into a full-sized house and we were now life-sized actors. Still inventing, we found a rocking chair, a rolltop desk, and a spinning wheel. . . . It felt like the *Twilight Zone*.

Paul Sills jumped up, excited! "That's it! That's *transformation*! That's what *we look for*! That's when *the magic happens*!" We never repeated that scene with a real audience. It was just a moment, an exciting moment . . . that I would never find again.

Even before Second City came to Broadway, an offshoot of improv theater opened in Greenwich Village on Bleecker Street. Ted Flicker, who had been associated with the Compass Players in Chicago, produced a show called *The Premise*. His actors included Gene Hackman, George Segal, Buck Henry, and others.

Later, in 1964, Elaine May took over that space with an improv group of her own. They were called The Third Ear. The actors were Peter Boyle, Mark Gordon, Renée Taylor, Louise Lasser, and others. I knew some of them and they were all talented, but because of my schedule I never got to see their show.

~

Many people find that speaking in public is one of their biggest fears. Doing it without a script worried me, too, but the more I improvised the easier it got.

After all, acting is no more than "pretending." Look at little kids, they "pretend" all the time. A cardboard crown makes a little girl a princess and a little boy a prince. They do all of this without ever taking a class in acting. It just comes naturally.

When actors study "improv" they play "games" to get back in touch with the child in themselves. It's even said that an actor "plays" his part . . . in a "play."

~

Kennedy was president, and the country had fallen in love with Jack and Jackie. Newspapers and magazines were full of stories. A young comedian named Vaughn Meader made a record, *The First Family*, doing a perfect impression of JFK. Sales of the record went through the roof. It made more money than any other spoken-word record ever and sold more than seven million copies.

At Second City there was a scene called "The Kennedy/Khrushchev Press Conference," where the two of them answered questions from the audience. Alan Arkin played Khrushchev using a gibberish Russian to answer questions. Sevren Darden would translate. On one occasion, Sevren said, "In answer to your question, Mr. Khrushchev quotes an old Russian proverb: 'When the owl screams in the forest . . . the hunter pisses on his foot.'" I had been given the part of President Kennedy. It wasn't hard to sound like him; every comic around was doing it. After the show one night, two writers asked me if I'd make a record album as JFK, probably trying to cash in on the Kennedy craze. They gave me the script and allowed me to contribute some jokes, and we made the record. They paid me $500. . . . I never heard from them again, nor ever heard the record.

~

One day, Sarah said to me, "You know, sometimes I wish you didn't make so much money." I thought, *Why would she say that?* It kinda stung me. As a father and a husband, I felt that doing well for myself meant doing well for the family. It was as if she felt we didn't deserve nice things . . . or *she* didn't.

Sarah decided to try therapy again. I thought, *Good. Maybe that doctor wasn't right for her, not a good fit, maybe a new therapist will be better.* I was hopeful. But before long she left that doctor as well.

I was still seeing Dr. K, who helped me understand some of the poor decisions I'd made and why I'd made them. I found these sessions helpful and continued working with him.

~

I was improvising with Second City six nights a week for a year. I started to wonder . . .

im·pro·vi·ser

/ˈɪm.prə.vaɪ.zɚ/

noun

An actor who performs without a script.

Was *that* me?

The fun of doing improv was that, if someone made a suggestion and the actors created a funny scene based on it, the person who made the suggestion felt like a partner in the success of the scene. Also, if they could see you were "making it up," and the scene failed, they were very forgiving. You got credit for even trying.

The company I had joined included a remarkable group of actors at the top of their game.

Andrew Duncan was a natural leader, the organized timekeeper, and the engine of the show. He has been called the "glue that held it all together." He had a keen intellect, and as an improviser he was one of the best.

Sevren Darden was, even offstage, a character. At the University of Chicago, he drove an old Rolls-Royce, often sporting a top hat and a cape. Well educated, and well read, he seemed to know everything about, well . . . everything. He was flamboyant, eccentric, and extremely funny, a kind of a genius, and sort of a madman.

Barbara Harris, the leading lady, was attractive, intelligent, and a good actress, often playing insecure and innocent young women, even teenagers with pathos and humor, and she had a commanding stage presence.

Mina Kolb, the other female, was adorable and endearing, and she always played a sort of vague and simplistic character. She was unflappable. Mina was the calm within the storm of the other improvisers.

Alan Arkin played many different characters, young and old, and was better at dialects than anyone, and he had an antic comic spirit. I was dazzled by his talent.

Eugene Troobnick also played a lot of different characters. He had a commanding delivery in everything he did and was a funny and versatile comic actor.

As the show gained popularity, so did our actors, and many of them were getting offers from elsewhere. Barbara left first to do a play, and Mina and Troobnick left for other jobs as well. Then Alan went to Broadway for *Enter Laughing*, after which he began a career in the movies.

Luckily, there were other improvisers waiting in the wings. The very beautiful Zorah Lampert from the Chicago company joined us for a while. MacIntyre Dixon, also from Chicago, arrived soon after. I knew and admired him from his work with Richard Libertini, and he became a great friend. Bob Dishy joined us and became the actor I would most often do scenes with. Bob was a fine physical actor as well. We'd often do silent scenes together.

Paul Sand had studied improvisation early at age eleven. He loved pantomime and preferred playing animals more than people. Paul was, by nature, shy. The characters he played were usually sweet and vulnerable. He had spent a year in Paris studying mime with Marcel Marceau.

Tony Holland was a big part of our company now. He had been improvising for several years in Chicago and was well prepared for the job. Tony knew literature, art history, languages, and mythology and often referenced them in his scenes. He was one of my favorites.

Not every scene we improvised was a winner, but from time to time, one of them was so good it became an instant classic, not a word needed to be changed. Tony Holland was the creator of one of those great scenes.

We had a standard scene, an interview with a celebrity. The audience suggested a female author. Tony said, "Let me do that." Tony was gay, and he thought he'd have fun with it . . . and he did. Here's the part I remember most.

He introduced himself/herself as Rhoda Shapiro and then spelled the name out. "Shapiro. That's S. C. H. A. E. P. I. R. O. E." He then added, "We're Portuguese."

That choice for that character, to me, was both priceless and hilarious.

Sad to say Tony passed away some years ago, but for me, he's still here and unforgettable.

~

Barbara Harris and I once walked onstage and asked the audience "Who are we?" We were told, "A husband and wife." "Anything special about us?" "The man does the cooking, the wife works." She left the stage. I assumed she wanted to take a moment backstage and then make an entrance. In the meantime, I began to put together a kitchen. This is called *creating* the "Where." As improvisers we were taught not only to invent our dialogue, but also to turn the stage into a real place; to try to make the invisible visible. I pantomimed turning on faucets, washing my hands, drying them, opening a window, looking through the cabinets. . . . Barbara was still offstage. I didn't mind, I was enjoying creating the "Where." I opened a fridge, got some eggs, found a bowl, cracked the eggs, stirred them up, still no Barbara. I turned on the stove, grabbed a frying pan, put the eggs in it, and was moving the handle back and forth to keep the eggs from sticking when Barbara entered:

"What are you doing?" she asked.

"I thought I'd scramble some eggs." I said.

"In a tennis racquet?"

The line got a huge laugh. To save face I said to her, "Oh . . . that's why the eggs kept falling in the fire." She had just broken the "first rule of improv": Listen and Agree. An actor never denies the other actor's reality. For an easy laugh, she had just pulled the rug out from under me . . . and the audience. Here's the deal. There's an unspoken contract with the audience. If they accept my words or my actions as reality, I won't undercut it just for a laugh. The truth is that any improviser will do this now and then, in a moment of weakness, or for an easy laugh . . . but it's best not to do it at all.

~

After *Enter Laughing*, Alan Arkin's career went into high gear. In a short time, he made three films. The first was *The Russians Are Coming, The Russians Are Coming*, where he played a Russian submarine captain with a dialect. He then appeared in Carson McCullers' *The Heart Is a Lonely Hunter* as a deaf man who never spoke. And in *Popi*, Alan played the title role with a Puerto Rican accent. I followed all these films, and in all of them, he was never less than brilliant.

~

Bob Dishy and I would often go onstage and play "transformations" in total silence. We would ask the audience to suggest an object, something you could hold in your hand. Frequently, they'd say, "A ball." We'd begin tossing an invisible baseball back and forth. Then one of us might enlarge it into, say, a basketball and start dribbling it. The other might take over the movement and turn it into . . . patting a kid on the head. And it would go on from there. If the suggestion had been a hand grenade, the scene would have gone in a completely different direction.

Some of the changes would get smiles or chuckles, and even big laughs if they were very inventive. I still remember a few inspired sequences.

Bob was pantomiming casting a fishing line, first throwing it out, then reeling it in, his hand moving back toward his shoulder. I copied the movement, and then, reaching over my shoulder, I pulled an arrow from a quiver, lined it up with my bow, and aimed it. Bob then took the bow and arrow and now he was aiming it as a rifle, which I then turned into a pool cue, which I was looking at to see if it was straight.

Bob and I enjoyed playing that game and liked surprising each other.

~

While I was in the show, I helped create some pretty good scenes. Most of them were funny but not all memorable . . . not exactly "classics." There were only two scenes that I could count as my best work. The Transformations with Dishy, and a scene I did with Alan Arkin in a dentist's office. I played the patient. The scene was totally silent, lasted about two minutes, and was extremely funny.

When Alan left us, I continued doing the scene, now playing the dentist, with Bob Dishy as my hapless patient. Over time we expanded the scene to six minutes, and it became, at least for Bob and me, a "classic." We were asked to do the scene on the Jack Paar TV show. I was finally doing the kind of silent comedy that Keaton had done.

My only other real accomplishment was with "Poetry." We would ask the audience for the first line of a poem that they would make up. We would take the first line and, one by one, we would improvise our own version of it. Some poems lasted, maybe, a minute or two, or even three, but because I had done Shakespearean parody in my nightclub act, I improvised my poem using that style. It involved a bit of what I would call "medieval-double-talk." On my first try I was getting such big laughs I did about five minutes. It continued to work well and was so dependable for getting laughs it kind of became my "thing." I did it off and on for a year in New York, and long after that I continued doing it with many other improv companies. Some of the characters I invented for it were "Scenario," "Portfolio," and "Fellatio." I called it . . . Fakespeare.

Second City was from Chicago (hence the name). The actors had honed their improvisation skills in an earlier group called Compass Players that did complete plays and one-acts and experimented with improv. Compass discovered and nourished Mike Nichols and Elaine May, clearly the best improvisers of them all (more about the two of them later).

Second City opened in 1959, and after more than sixty years, it is still going strong. Thousands of comic actors started there, and hundreds of them became stars.

Beyond Chicago, the improv revolution spread to Toronto, where the cast included John Candy, Eugene Levy, Martin Short, Catherine O'Hara, Andrea Martin, Dave Thomas, and Rick Moranis, all of whom moved on to the series SCTV (originally titled *Second City TV*). *SNL* found its original cast mostly from Second City. Among them were John Belushi, Dan Ackroyd, Gilda Radner, and Bill Murray.

Soon colleges started teaching improv. The book most often used was *Improvisation for the Theater* by Viola Spolin, Paul Sills's mother and the pathfinder of improv.

Eventually, there were hundreds of improv troupes in cities everywhere.

23
Sixty-Second Stories

Our Second City company appeared on a two-hour TV show using all the best sketches. That show was being talked about all over New York. Madison Avenue came calling. They wanted that kind of wit and satire in their commercials. Of course, I was already known in that world for my on-camera work, but the ad agencies wanted us for radio spots.

I began working with Andrew Duncan. He was fast on his feet, quick with a quip . . . and, as it turned out, I was too. We were put together so many times doing funny radio spots we became a team.

At first the scripts were already written (and not too funny). Andrew and I would throw a few lines in, improving the script. We got very busy, doing those radio spots several times a week.

After about six months, some of the ad agencies were repeat customers. Andy and I knew we were making the scripts better but only being paid as actors, not as writers. Just because we were improvising didn't mean we weren't writing; we were just writing out loud without a pencil. So, we asked for a creative fee of $25 each for our contributions. The ad agencies agreed.

As our radio spots became more and more popular, we would increase the creative fee. Soon we would be making more as writers than as actors. We decided to ask if we could just create radio spots from scratch. The ad men would only have to give us their message and we'd do the rest. We

My partner, Andrew Duncan. Quick with a quip and fast on his feet. AUTHOR'S COLLECTION.

got organized, named our new business All Over Creation, and began doing a series of spots *all our own*. Here's an excerpt from one of our favorites:

Announcer: "Burlington presents a little history with the Wright Brothers."
"Ready Orville?"
"Ready Wilbur!"
"How do you feel?"
"Great! . . . I think today's the day we make aviation history."
"What's aviation?"
"Never mind . . . but it is a special day, that's why I decided to wear worsted."
"What's worsted?"
"This suit . . . it's worsted wool. Wool made the worsted way."
"Looks sharp."
"That's because it holds its shape so well. When I land this aeroplane, I want to be dressed in my best."
"So you dressed in your worsted."
"Right."
"That's what I call flying first class."
"Wilbur, when you're Wright, you're right!"
"Oh, Brother!"

One of my favorite lines I ever improvised in a radio spot was when our client was General Motors Acceptance Corporation (or just GMAC). We decided to fill the spot with other acronyms like ASAP, FYI, and AWOL. We did a lot of them, so when Andy said, "and if you act now, you'll get a 10 percent discount," I surprised him by saying, "Why didn't you tell me that initially?"

As much fun as I was having improvising with Andrew, I found nothing lighthearted at home. Sarah seemed sometimes depressed or worried. One day, she seemed more stressed than usual, and I wasn't sure why.

Then there was this telling incident. Her father would sometimes come from the Midwest to visit us in Brooklyn for a few days. I liked him. He was a very nice man.

Hours before his next arrival, Sarah said to me, in a desperate tone, "I can't see him! I don't want him here! Tell him anything! I don't care!" I didn't understand what was happening. I thought maybe there had been a phone call or a letter, or some unresolved issue between them that had come to the surface. I headed him off and tried to put a good face on everything. I explained that she was feeling overwhelmed right now. I got a hotel room for him; we had a meal together. That's the last time he came to visit.

24
A Dream Come True

So, I get this call, and the agent says, "There's a commercial to be filmed in the style of a silent movie. Are you interested?" "Am I interested?" I said. "I've got to be in it!" I arranged a meeting with the producer and brought along photos from my silent films. I got the job. I was to play a Keystone Cop, who, along with several others, would be chasing some baggy-pants comedian. Then I learned that the comedian would be . . .

Who was that again? Oh, Buster Keaton . . . *Buster Keaton? Oh my God!* I couldn't believe it!!

On the day, there he was . . . the man himself . . . older now, in his seventies, but unmistakably Buster, flat hat and all. Actors are told not to talk to stars, to just give them their space and do your job. Besides, I was too overwhelmed to say anything. The commercial was for Ford Econoline Vans. The cops would be chasing Buster in and out and around a number of them. Between takes he would lie down on the grass nearby with his flat hat over his face taking catnaps.

There was, luckily for me, a second day of filming. At the end of day one, I approached the great man and shyly asked him, "If I bring a book you've written, and a photo, would you autograph them?" He said, "Sure."

The first word I had ever heard him speak.

I still have that book, and the photo is framed on my wall. Every time I look at it, I smile.

25
Oscar and Felix and Mike

I was booked to do a commercial live on *The Today Show*. At that time on the program, you would see tourists on the street through a big window, often holding up signs with the names of their hometowns on them. I was there too, dressed as Santa Claus and holding up a sign saying "Samsonite," then holding up the actual suitcase. I didn't say anything, *The Today Show* host did all the talking.

I would be seen on TV at about 8:00 a.m. I rehearsed my part at 6:00 a.m. and then had two hours to wait. They gave me a tiny dressing room. How was I going to kill two hours? I didn't have a book to read, but I did have three or four pages for an audition at noon that day. It was for *The Odd Couple*, and it was going to be a big deal. Neil Simon wrote the play and Mike Nichols (by the way, that's *the* Mike Nichols) would direct it. I started learning my lines. I would be trying out for the part of a poker player, but since that part had only scattered lines here and there, I had been told to audition by reading the part of Felix Unger. The character was neat, tidy, and fussy.

Soon I knew all of Felix's lines and started memorizing my cues, which another character, Oscar, would be saying. I had so much time, and nothing else to do, I got all the lines down cold. I was totally prepared.

I went to the theater and was brought onstage. Even though I knew all the lines, it's always a good idea to hold the script in case you get nervous and forget. There was a moment, halfway through the scene, where Felix is annoyed with Oscar, and since I was so secure with my words, I used that moment to throw my script away, high over my head (it's always funny to see something important thrown away). Now the pages were all over the floor, which allowed me, as Felix, to get down on

123

my knees and pick them up while continuing with the dialogue (which was totally in character for Felix). That got a big laugh.

Mike thanked me, and I headed for the exit. I felt I had done well. It's normal, after an audition, to wait until your agent calls to say, "You got it!" (or "You didn't."), but that day, the stage manager came running after me, yelling, "You got it!" Was I excited? Were the Dark Ages hard to read by? I called my agent to give him the news. He said, "Congratulations!" and told me he'd get the date when rehearsals began. Then he added, "Oh, by the way, call Joe Hamilton. He wants to talk to you."

Joe Hamilton was the producer of Carol Burnett's show, *The Entertainers*, and also, her husband. Of course, I had already been on that show a few times. Joe told me that, instead of joining them now and then, he'd like me to be a regular cast member and appear on every show. You can imagine my dilemma: two big shows I wanted to be a part of but could take only one.

I explained to Joe that I had just been offered a role in *The Odd Couple* and felt I had to take it. Simon and Nichols were very hot at that time. Their other comedy, *Barefoot in the Park*, starring Robert Redford, was a huge hit, still running on Broadway, and I felt the new play might just run for years. Joe said, "You know, I think you're right. Congratulations!"

At our first rehearsal, Mike Nichols said, "This play is not a comedy, there are no jokes, so don't go for laughs. Neil Simon has already taken care of that, just play the scenes for real . . . the laughs will come." He also said, "I don't want you poker players to *pretend* to play the game, I want it to be a real game. If there are quiet moments in the play, I want to hear a game. Your lines can be muted but I want it to be real."

As rehearsals proceeded the card players would be given a three-hour lunch break while Mike worked with the two stars. Because, as it turned out, I was also going to be the understudy for Art Carney, who would be playing Felix, I stayed there to hear all his lines over and over so I could learn them by listening. Walter Matthau would play Oscar Madison.

I would sit at the back of the theater as Mike Nichols talked to his stars. I couldn't make out what they were saying, but I'd be taking notes on the moves that the actors were making. Even though I was far away, I noticed that Art Carney was just what you'd expect him to be, the lovable, loopy sewer-specialist Ed Norton from Jackie Gleason's *The Honeymooners*, but that was just his "TV persona." Privately, Art was a shy, quiet, even modest fellow, and in the words of Michael Seth Starr's *Art Carney: A Biography*, "he was happy to blend into the woodwork."

According to Starr, "Matthau was known for his laconic demeanor and his hang-dog, world-weary expression." Next to Carney, he was hardly the funnier of the two, but it seemed as if Walter needed to be the center of attention.

After four weeks, we left New York to "try out" the play out of town. For six weeks on the road, Simon and Nichols were fine-tuning the play. Act 1 was never a problem, it worked like a charm . . . but the ending of Act 2 was a different story. Simon had to rewrite new versions of the last scene many, many times until he found one that worked.

Finally, we opened on Broadway. The critics *raved!* The show was a *smash! . . . A palpable hit!* One of the critics said, "Recently, the Moscow Art Theatre played the City Center in New York doing a play by Chekhov. Those actors could learn something from the poker players in *The Odd Couple.* That was real ensemble acting." Thank you, Mike!

I had never been in a Broadway show and was so starstruck that, for the first month, I would look through the peephole in the curtain (most Broadway theaters have one) and make a list of celebrities.

There was Robert Redford, Jack Lemmon, Elaine May, Danny Kaye, Carol Channing, Jack Benny, George Burns, and Bert Lahr. There were also composer Leonard Bernstein and director Elia Kazan. At some point later on, a backstage visitor was Senator Robert Kennedy.

A sign of the times . . . a ticket to the play cost $17.25.

~

Since every actor had an understudy, we'd have rehearsals once a week to make sure we were ready to fill in when needed. When we were previewing the show out of town, Art Carney never missed a performance, but after three weeks of playing on Broadway, Art didn't show up one night. He didn't call in to warn us, he just did not show up. This was unheard of. Showing up a half hour before curtain was the golden rule. When he missed, at the last minute, I quickly put on my Felix costume and played the part. I wasn't nervous, I knew all my lines, got all my laughs (not surprisingly, since Neil Simon's lines were so surefire funny).

The next day I got a call from an agent at the William Morris Agency. That agency was the biggest in show business, representing hundreds of actors. He said to me, "Walter Matthau is our client and tells us you replaced Art Carney last night. He said you did very well, that you have a lot of talent and should have a successful career ahead of you. We're wondering if you have representation?" (That's agent-talk for do you have an agent?) I told him that I did. He asked, "Who are you with?" I said, "You guys!"

Of course, I'd been with the Morris Agency for over a year, but it's such a huge organization he'd never heard of me. Anyway, I thought, *That was nice of Walter Matthau.*

~

On a Sunday, my day off, my son Adam was born, and he was just as adorable as Robin. Since he was my firstborn son, his name came from the Bible . . . (not that I'm God or anything).

I'll share with you a secret about me . . . I had always had the feeling that no one would ever love me. But once Robin was born, and now with Adam, I knew that my children would always love me as I loved

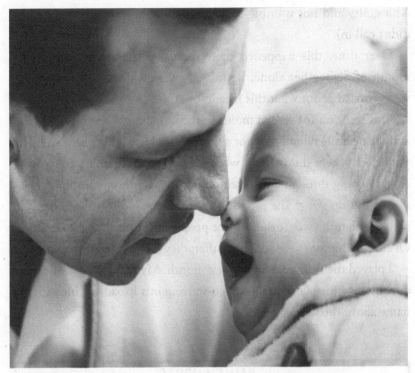

My first-born son, Adam. We could not be any closer. BOB ROSS

them . . . and they would *always* be a part of my life. Just knowing that Adam and Robin would be there when I came home at night from the play made me anxious to get there. Looking in on them as they lay innocently sleeping was so rewarding.

~

My going on for Art Carney became a fairly regular thing. About every week he'd miss a show; but he never warned us. I was getting even more sure of myself in making the role my own.

It soon became clear that Art had a drinking problem. Those times when he couldn't do the show, the cast thought he was probably in a bar nearby but felt he was not sober enough to go on (maybe, feeling a bit guilty and not wanting to lie about why he'd be missing, he just didn't call in).

Over time, this happened more often. As Starr tells us, "In the month of September alone, he missed twelve shows." The producers were worried about what this meant.

This went on for several months. Then, one night, he missed again, and the next night, and then for a third night. He couldn't be reached by phone. His agent didn't know where he was; his wife didn't even know. Art was going through a divorce and not living at home. I thought, *No wonder he's drinking!* The producers were in a panic. Art was a big star, and any night he wasn't there, some people asked for their money back. Of course, the show itself did not suffer; they just wanted their star back.

I played the Felix role for about a month. My name was on the marquee along with Matthau's. I was co-starring in a Broadway hit with my name above the title.

SAINT SUBBER

presents

WALTER MATTHAU   PAUL DOOLEY

in

NEIL SIMON'S New Comedy

THE ODD COUPLE

Directed by

MIKE NICHOLS

Program from *The Odd Couple*. I was now, oddly, a part of the couple. USED BY PERMISSION. ALL RIGHTS RESERVED, PLAYBILL, INC.

During this time, a strange thing happened. My agent began getting calls from Los Angeles. Suddenly there was a lot of interest in me from the networks. There were about a dozen offers for leading roles in TV sitcoms.

It was "pilot season," where one episode of a new show is filmed (the pilot), to see if it will become a series or not. I thought all this interest in me was because I was playing a leading role on Broadway.

I turned down all these offers since I was already co-starring in a hit show. Then the producers told me that Carney wasn't coming back. He had gone to a clinic to "dry out." They also told me they had found a new star to replace him. Naturally, I was disappointed (and just a little pissed off). I thought I had been doing a great job in the show, but it seems they felt they needed a "name" for that role, and I was not a "name." The new Felix would be Eddie Bracken, a well-known, very likeable actor who had played comic parts in movies in the past.

They told me I could return to my place at the poker table. I felt that after a year with the show, and getting to play Felix with some success, it just didn't feel right to me. I said, "No thanks, I'll be moving on."

Still, all in all, I had a great time in *The Odd Couple*.

I learned later that all of the excitement about me for sitcoms had nothing to do with *The Odd Couple*. It turns out I'd made a commercial for Kent cigarettes, which was very popular, and in which I had a lot of close-ups. It had played during the Oscars and everybody in Hollywood had seen me. Oh, well. *The Odd Couple* was only on Broadway, but commercials were everywhere.

~

A quick story about the Kent cigarette commercial. My agent called to ask, "Do you smoke?" I told her yes. Actors will often lie about skills they don't really have (like horseback riding). The actor would audition for the job, and then, if he was hired, he'd take a few lessons.

Of course, I had never smoked and knew that, at the audition, I might cough and ruin the moment. I went out and bought a pack of Kents, came home and started practicing. Naturally, I coughed for a while but then relaxed, took my time, and taught myself to inhale. So far so good.

At the audition, I decided to inhale only once, smile, then look at the cigarette, so mesmerized by it, that I seemed to be making love, visually, to the cigarette.

Everyone loved it!

I got the job. I faked my way through the filming. My fear of inhaling and coughing had accidentally created a popular commercial.

The character's name was Harvey. People on the street started calling me that. Cab drivers would say, "You're Harvey!" I'd say, "Yes, I am." "And you smoke Kents!" and I'd answer . . . "Yes . . . but I'm trying to quit."

26
Breaking the Fourth Wall

This book was never meant to be a "tell-all" about other actors, but I will share with you my experience of working with Walter Matthau.

To begin with, he was a wonderful Oscar Madison, he was born to play the part. Oscar is a divorced man living alone who lets a friend, Felix, whose wife has kicked him out, move in with him. Little did he know how hard his life would become. Felix is neat . . . very, very neat. Oscar is sloppy . . . very, very sloppy. The crux of the play is how they drive each other crazy.

During our New York rehearsals there were no problems. On the first night on our out-of-town tryout, we were in Boston (Sarah had come to see the show). Now we had a live audience. Oscar, annoyed at Felix, was supposed to look toward heaven and plead, "Why doesn't he hear me? I know I'm talking. I recognize my voice." A surefire laugh. Instead, Matthau picked out someone in the front row of the audience and asked the question of him. He got a huge laugh, as he knew he would.

In the theater there's an expression, "Never break the fourth wall." The unspoken rule is that when an actor looks out toward the audience, he does not see them, he sees only an invisible fourth wall, which may have a painting on it, a bookcase, a forest, or even an ocean.

After the play, the actors gathered onstage to get "notes" from the director. Mike Nichols said to Matthau, "When you broke the fourth wall you got your laugh, but it was a cheap laugh at the expense of the play. We lose the audience, and it might take us ten minutes to get them back."

Matthau said, "I'm sorry, Mike. . . . It just came out." Nichols said, "Fine, but it's not a good idea." At the next performance he did it again.

Another big laugh, another note, another excuse, and for weeks Matthau continued defying the director's word, and Nichols still gave the same note, and Matthau still had a lame excuse. He would not give up his big laugh. It was like a war. An actor normally listens to what the director says . . . except, of course, when he doesn't.

Once we opened on Broadway, Mike Nichols was gone and now the actors were on their own . . . and Matthau continued to get his big laugh.

There's a reason why Walter was so competitive with Art Carney. Art was a much bigger star than Matthau, his salary was more than double Walter's, and after the show many, many people lined up backstage to meet Art Carney. Not so many for Matthau. Might he have been just a little jealous?

It's true that the part of Oscar was a better showcase than the part of Felix was. Simon had supplied Oscar with actual jokes . . . "Felix wears a seatbelt at a drive-in movie." In fact, the biggest laugh in the show was Matthau's: "You leave me little notes on my pillow. 'We are all out of cornflakes . . . F.U.' Took me three hours to figure out that F.U. was Felix Ungar!"

Felix's laughs, on the other hand, were all character-driven, based on behavior, not jokes, so it was not surprising that Matthau would, as Starr's book tells us, "Win a Tony Award . . . while Art, critically praised, didn't even merit a nomination."

Matthau was an experienced stage performer who knew about "upstaging," a term used to describe where the actors stand in relationship to each other. If two actors are doing a scene, both in profile, and one actor moves a step away from the audience (or upstage), this forces his fellow actor to turn a little to continue the scene. When this happens, the audience will now see the back of the head of the poor actor who didn't make the move . . . very clever, Walter, but very selfish.

There's also a term in theater called "milking." It means when an actor has a big moment (either dramatic or comic) and tries to extend it to win the audience's approval by doing even more, or "milking the moment." This will often be a "crowd pleaser." However, when the scene is no longer about the character in the play but more about the actor "stepping outside the play" for his own gratification, then it goes "too far" and hurts the play. Matthau was a master of this.

Carney, who was a much nicer guy, never complained about this, but all of us other actors could see it and felt for him. The poker players were, according to Starr's biography, "becoming increasingly irritated with Matthau's onstage shenanigans, which not only disrupted Art's timing, but also jangled the other actors' nerves."

Month after month this went on. Each night when we were offstage, we complained to one another about Walter's behavior. The stage manager finally called a meeting after a matinee performance to tell us, "I've noticed a problem with the company's morale. There has been a lot of gossip and grumbling in the wings, comments onstage, changing lines, so what's going on?"

There was a long silence. None of the complaining poker players said a word. . . . Art said nothing. I surprised myself by speaking up; it was the first time I had ever confronted anyone. "The problem is that Walter is fucking up the play every night." Again, silence. Matthau began his excuses. "Well, I like to kid around. It relaxes me. It helps my performance, maybe if you all feel this way, maybe you should get another actor." Yeah, sure, keep this complaining actor and replace the big star.

The meeting broke up, and nothing had been decided. We all went out to dinner. When we came back for the evening show, the stage manager came to my dressing room to say, "Mr. Matthau would like to see you in his dressing room." I said, "Tell Mr. Matthau to go fuck himself." I never heard another word about it.

That being said, I had made my point, but nothing changed, Since I was just the understudy, I "put up" with Matthau's bad behavior. But once I was playing Felix for good, I wouldn't let Walter *get away* with his bullshit . . . now I could "upstage" him, too.

He began to be a bit more respectful.

One day, Sarah said to me, "I can see you've made some progress with your therapist. Maybe I could work with him. What do you think?" Sharing an analyst isn't usually recommended. I told her that I'd ask my doctor, and if it was okay with him, it would be okay with me. I even thought it might help.

After a few months with Dr. K, a man who knew not only *my* side of our story but her side as well, she walked out on him too. She told me, "I'm tired of all these doctors. Maybe therapy can't help some people."

I began to think maybe the problem wasn't all those therapists, maybe it was her. Maybe every time one of her doctors came too close to something painful in her past, she had to escape.

All these episodes with therapists didn't happen in a single year. They continued over some time, and we weren't getting anywhere with our underlying problems. Since we had trouble communicating, I thought therapy was our only hope.

~

In 1968, Dom DeLuise was given his own TV variety show. Having known Dom from *The Entertainers*, I was asked to join his company of sketch players. The other performers were Marian Mercer and Bill McCutcheon, both terrific comic actors. Our family picked up and went to Miami for the summer.

We settled in at a very nice apartment with a pool and a playground for the kids. I was rehearsing every day. At first, things seemed fine with Sarah, but before long, with little to do but sit by the pool while the kids swam, she seemed to become bored. For Robin and Adam this was a vacation; but not for her. She appeared to be unhappy. She didn't complain, so we didn't talk about it, but, again, it seemed we weren't communicating.

From *A Wedding* with Carol Burnett and Mia Farrow. My first film with Robert Altman. TWENTIETH CENTURY FOX FILM CORP./PHOTOFEST ©TWENTIETH CENTURY FOX FILM CORP.

With Dennis Christopher and Barbara Barrie, just after winning the big race in *Breaking Away*. AUTHOR'S COLLECTION.

Olive Oyl, Wimpy, and Popeye watching as Bluto kidnaps Baby Sweetpea.

Molly and me in *Sixteen Candles* . . . my best remembered "Movie Dad."

Winnie and I on our wedding day. I loved that my kids were there. AUTHOR'S COLLECTION.

Runaway Bride with Julia Roberts. I'm the dad and I drink too much.

With Al Pacino in *Insomnia*. Al played a troubled cop and Robin Williams was the bad guy. AUTHOR'S COLLECTION.

Wicked artwork and logo. WICKED ARTWORK AND LOGO ™ ©®
WICKED LLC. ALL RIGHTS RESERVED.

Sarge from *Cars*. An old-time Jeep with an old guy's voice. ©DISNEY/
PIXAR

On the set of *Hairspray*. My scenes were all with Michelle Pfeiffer, but John Travolta was nice enough to pose for this candid snapshot. AUTHOR'S COLLECTION.

Winnie and Savannah on the set of *HUGE*. AMERICAN BROADCASTING COM-PANIES, INC. ALL RIGHTS RESERVED.

"Star Trek: Deep Space 9" I played Enabran Tain. He was a real bastard, but fun to play. AUTHOR'S COLLECTION.

Winnie and Claire Danes on the set of *My So-Called Life*. AUTHOR'S COLLECTION.

"The Country House," my first oil painting. AUTHOR'S COLLECTION.

27
A New Voice

Eventually, Andrew and I added a new voice to our radio spots. In fact, a lot of new voices. They belonged to the very funny Lynne Lipton.

Andrew and I had one voice each. Lynne had a ton of them, and she could also improvise. Andrew and I were always just two guys talking about some product; adding a woman's voice to the mix meant we could do more commercials for products appealing to women. We began to get even more work.

I spoke to an executive from a company called Martin Paint. He wasn't sure but said he might want a humorous radio spot for his chain of paint stores. I gave him a bargain rate for one commercial. I told him, "Just pay the two of us as actors and add $100 each for the writing."

He explained his problem to me. The company sold lots and lots of paint, but their customers weren't aware of all the other things they

Versatile Lynne Lipton. When she "heard voices" they were usually her own. AUTHOR'S COLLECTION.

sold. "I can help you with that!" I said. "Once they hear the commercial, they'll never forget what Martin Paint is all about."

Lynne and I recorded what turned out to be our most popular, most long-running, and most prizewinning radio spot ever. It was on for years.

"Uh . . . Ms. Grimble?"

"Yes?"

"Welcome to Martin Paint."

"Thank you."

"Since this is your first day, I thought I'd help you get started."

"Oh, good!"

"Uh . . . this is your switchboard."

"Oh, I recognized it right away."

"Ah, good!"

"Oh, this is really a big place."

"Well, the Martin Home Decorating Centers are quite extensive."

"My!"

Phone rings.

"Oh, there's your first call."

"Good morning! Welcome to Martin Paint . . . uh, no, I'm sorry."

Hangs up.

"Uh, what was that?"

"Wall coverings."

"Oh, we have wall coverings!"

"Oh."

"Over sixteen hundred patterns."

"Really?"

"And floor coverings. All the national brands."

"My!"

"Be careful."

Phone rings.

"Good morning! Martin Paint. Floor coverings and wall coverings. . . . No, I'm sorry."

Hangs up.

"Uh, what was that?"
"Decorative lumber."
"Oh, Ms. Grimble. Look around you. What do you see?"
"Decorative lumber . . ."
"That's right! This is a complete home decorating center."
"Oh . . ."
"Ceiling tiles, wall tiles, cork tiles, mirror tiles, lighting fixtures, dimmers, bulbs . . ."
"But I can't say all that!"
"Well, do the best you can."

Phone rings.

"Good morning! Martin Home Decorating Centers . . . *It Ain't Just Paint!*"

Once the radio spot went on the air, it "caught on" and played constantly. Martin Paint put that catchphrase on *every bucket of paint*, on *all their trucks*, and in *all* their *newspaper ads*.

"It Ain't Just Paint" became a thing in New York. A fast-food place on 42nd Street, which sold chicken, added burgers to the menu and put up a sign: "It Ain't Just Chicken." A hair salon on Long Island added manicures with a sign claiming: "It Ain't Just Hair." I thought this copycat thing was hilarious. The only thing "It Ain't Just Paint" had going for it was the rhyme. Without it, what was the point?

28
Elaine

My agent tells me, "They're holding auditions for a Broadway show and are looking for improvisers." He said, "They're only seeing a few people." When I got to the theater, I found a very big crowd of actors (anyone who had ever *seen* an improv show was there). Nobody knew what this was all about.

A producer explained to us that Mort Sahl, the very popular comedian, was about to do a Broadway show; he'd already done a successful one-man show on Broadway earlier. This time he wanted to add a small group of actors to help him expand his comedy ideas. Then he introduced . . . Elaine May.

I was excited just to be in the same room with her. She said, "Pick someone you want to work with." I picked Bill Fiore and Carol Morley, both friends of mine from the world of commercials. Small scraps of paper were handed out telling the actors what scene they'd be improvising. Ours told us we would be actors at an audition for a TV commercial. What a perfect assignment! The three of us had been in that exact situation hundreds of times. We improvised the scene.

The next day we were told we'd been hired, and we met with Elaine at the theater. She explained that our job would be to "play out" short scenes that Mort Sahl had just set up in his monologues. Mort Sahl was not there.

The next day we met with Elaine again and workshopped improv scenes to get the actors more acquainted with each other as improvisers. She told us one of Mort Sahl's ideas: A man is living his life on a game board. She thought it could make a funny scene. Again, Mort Sahl was not there.

The following day when we met, Elaine had a script for us to look at. It was her version of the game board idea, but instead of a scene lasting three or four minutes, she had gotten carried away and, overnight, had written an entire one-act play nearly an hour long about the guy on the game board. She called it "Adaptation." We read it aloud, and it was brilliant! But, of course it was. Elaine May wrote it.

A few hours later the producer showed up with the news that Mort Sahl could not be found. He had apparently left town, the whole thing would be canceled, and there would be no show.

Sometime later, in 1969, it all came to life again. We went into rehearsal with Elaine directing.

I had already read every article and every book about Elaine. I had also talked with the actors who had improvised with her at the Compass Players. She was sometimes described as a "nightmare." My experience with her was just the opposite. Not only was she not a nightmare, she was great with her actors, and we all loved her. Those comments about her were all made by men who were probably intimidated by Elaine, finding her smarter and more talented than they were, maybe even jealous of her.

I had also heard that she didn't care, at all, about how she looked. That part was true. During our four-week rehearsal, she wore the same uniform every day . . . a dark navy peacoat. If the ash on her cigarette grew longer and longer, it just fell off onto her coat. She was so focused on the work we were doing, nothing else mattered.

Once, there was an interview in a magazine, and the reporter asked Elaine, "What's the most important thing to you as an actress?" And Elaine said . . . "Grooming." That made me laugh.

With "Adaptation," there was no scenery. The set was just a game board painted on the floor, kind of like Monopoly. A narrator tells the leading actor (and the audience) how the game will proceed. "You have failed Puberty, go back two spaces." I played every man he'd ever known in his life. His father, his son, his analyst, his professor, and so on, and Carol Morley played every woman he had ever met.

We had not been told exactly how to move around the stage; this is what's called "blocking." Carol asked Elaine about how she should move, and Elaine said, "Just do whatever Paul's doing. *I hate blocking.*" Of course, she hated blocking . . . she and Mike had been sitting on stools forever . . . never moving.

We opened Off-Broadway, now paired with another one-act play, *Next*, by Terrence McNally. It was well received, and it ran for a year and a half.

Working with that genius, Elaine May, is one of my fondest memories.

29
Marriage at a Crossroad

I found myself living in two worlds. By day I would enjoy working with my friends creating comedy and then return home where tensions with my wife were in sharp contrast to my day job. I couldn't get her to tell me what was wrong. It seemed she didn't even like me anymore; maybe she thought I wasn't the same person she had married, that I'd changed. Maybe I had. I just felt completely in the dark.

One evening I was working until around 5:30 p.m. I called to say I'd be home in twenty minutes. I took the subway to Brooklyn. On the walk home a young man stopped me. He had seen me in Second City and went on and on about how he had enjoyed my comedy. Well, like most actors, I enjoy getting compliments, so the conversation went on for a while.

When I got home, I was twenty minutes late. Sarah had finished dinner. As I was taking my coat off, she walked into the kitchen with my dinner plate, now cold, I guessed. But instead of handing it to me, she dropped it on the floor. The plate broke. There was food all over the place. I picked up the broken pieces and cleaned up the floor. I could see it was my fault for being late, but . . . it seemed it wasn't just about the plate or being late. There was clearly something more that was bothering her . . . maybe the last nine years.

I felt that without help she was not going to be able to solve her problems . . . our problems. Or if it turned out *I was the problem*, it might be better for both of us if I moved out. I certainly didn't want to leave my kids, but I thought there was something wrong with our marriage that neither of us, nor an army of analysts could fix. So . . . I decided to leave.

One of the hardest moments I had ever experienced was telling my kids. I spoke to them both briefly, telling them that their mom and I were mad at each other right now, so I was going someplace else to live for a while, but that I would see them soon. I hugged each of them and told them I loved them and left.

I sat in my car for a while, then broke down . . . and cried.

~

Sarah and I agreed on a schedule of visits I'd have with the kids. I would take them for three out of four weekends, giving her a break, and an occasional weekday sleepover with one or both of them. I could have taken them to the country house, but it was winter, and I was living in a hotel. I switched to a larger room with two beds and an extra cot and asked the kids to bring a few toys to keep there.

I enjoyed my visits with them, but it all felt a little *artificial*. The kids weren't in their own home. Hell, I wasn't even in my own home. There was a lot of park, a lot of zoo, but it must have been a very confusing time for them. . . . I know it was for me. When you're used to being with them every day, it was hard not having that. Sometimes, when there was a sleepover, after we had had our dinner, they'd fall asleep. They looked so beautiful then, so innocent. I'd often just watch them sleep for a while. Watching them like that was just another way of being with them.

When I left home, I wasn't sure if I'd come back at some point. I continued to send Sarah money, took over household expenses, and left our station wagon with her. I bought a used car for myself.

My wife and I would get together from time to time and try to "work things out," but nothing ever seemed to get "worked out." It did not look promising.

Over time, there was less and less communication, and finally it stopped altogether. Just a few notes given to me by the kids about medications and things like that.

Robin and Adam at the
Brooklyn House. AUTHOR'S
COLLECTION.

~

The separation lasted for a few years. The kids were getting older,
becoming more who they would be someday.

The two of them were a lot alike: both were shy, both were kind of
vulnerable. Robin was very thoughtful; she seemed even wise for her
age. I felt a sense of inner strength about her.

Adam was more open, more playful. He reminded me a little of
myself at his age, and he had a sunny disposition and an innocent half
smile that I found endearing.

~

Finally, I received a notice from her lawyer that she was suing me for
divorce. I found a lawyer for myself. Eventually, it was settled, and the
divorce became final. The city house was now hers; the country house
was mine. I would also be paying alimony, child support, the mort-
gage each month, and tuition for private school. I was able to arrange
for a generous visitation schedule. My lawyer asked for a clause in our
divorce agreement that Sarah would not move more than fifty miles

from New York City. Although she agreed to those terms, I realize now that it may have seemed to her that I was trying to control her life.

Well, now I had been divorced twice. With the first marriage, I didn't think "husband" defined me, but after two divorces I thought that might be who I am . . . or was.

hus·band

/ˈhəz-bənd/

noun

A male partner in a marriage; a married man.

But if it was who I was, I wasn't very good at it.

~

At times my work would take me to LA, usually for TV shows. When that happened, I would need to cancel a visit or two with the kids. This upset my ex-wife, since she would then have to change her own plans. I understood her frustration but didn't know what else I could do. I could hardly take the kids out of school, fly them to LA, leave them with a hotel babysitter while I was at work, then fly them home. Because of the expenses of the divorce, I had to keep working. The court had said that my visits with the kids were a privilege, not an obligation. It was an unfortunate set of circumstances I couldn't change.

~

Divorced but still tied to my ex-wife through our kids, and feeling unable to discuss anything with her, made it difficult to navigate those visits. Since Sarah was so strict about schedules, I would often arrive fifteen minutes early and sit in the car until the kids came out.

Once, I arrived ten minutes late for a pickup because there had been a traffic jam on the Brooklyn Bridge. She told me I was too late, and they had gone to a playdate at their friend's house.

I was angry, and for the first time, I spoke to her very forcefully. *"Have them come home right now! I'm not leaving without them!"*

She went upstairs, I assumed to call the kids. Within five minutes the cops arrived and took me down to the station. I explained what had happened, and they understood my situation. They took me back to the house and told her she needed to let me take the kids for our visit.

I drove away with them that day on our trip to the country house. The kids seemed subdued, serious. They seemed to be bringing their mother's anxiety with them. Partway through the trip they began to relax more. By the time we got to the house, they jumped out of the car, now in a very good mood.

On the way home the reverse happened. Starting out carefree and happy, with every mile they prepared themselves to go home appearing not to have enjoyed the weekend. It was sad to see.

Once, we were driving home during winter. We had left at 4:30 p.m. and were due back in Brooklyn at 6:30 p.m. The trip usually took an hour and twenty minutes; we had left early. Half an hour into our ride it started snowing. Pretty soon there was a foot of snow, traffic was crawling along at twenty miles per hour, and I was already going to be late. Then, my windshield wipers stopped working. I couldn't get them started.

I'm not a car guy. I barely know what's under the hood, but I knew I had to do something. I pulled over. Now I was not just trying to meet my ex-wife's deadlines; I just didn't want to run out of gas and have us all freeze to death.

I went to my trunk and found some heavy-duty twine. I tied the twine to the windshield wiper, then put it through the window, pulled it across and out the other window, then tied it, on the outside, to the other wiper. I closed the windows, leaving a tiny opening for the twine.

I now had a loop of twine, and while driving with one hand, I used the other hand to move the wipers back and forth and manually made them work.

We made it home an hour late. I don't know what the kids told their mom. I didn't care. I never heard a word about it.

~

Silence from my ex-wife continued. I knew nothing about her; friends of mine told me they had heard her on radio programs talking about men holding women back from their true potential. I agreed with the new feminist agenda, but her abrupt change still surprised me. She had apparently become an ardent feminist but had never discussed these ideas with me.

Sarah was a few years younger than me. We had both grown up in the 1930s and 1940s and were living out an unwritten script where men were expected to work, earn a salary, and provide for their families, while women were expected to marry, have children, and stay at home with them. I think Sarah felt her family expected that of her, but in her heart of hearts I think she wanted more. She was an actress, a singer, a piano player, and she even took dance classes. That all seemed to end when she became a mother, but that way of thinking was changing. Women were demanding more for themselves, and it seemed Sarah might have had . . . an awakening.

30
See Spot. See Spot Run. Run Spot Run.

The call was from the Children's Television Workshop. I thought maybe they wanted me to do a voice for *Sesame Street*. I was very familiar with the show since I often watched it with my kids. It was the only children's show I had ever seen that was kinda hip, mainly because of the Muppets, who were, frankly, hilarious.

At the meeting, the producers, Sam Gibbon and Dave Conner, told me that they would be creating a new show to help kids learn to read. Our target audience would be between seven and ten years old.

They had a seven-million-dollar budget for the first season. I was impressed. *Seven million dollars . . .* I thought, *That's a lot of money.* They offered me a job. I signed on. The next day I told a friend of mine, "After all this time doing all those commercials, just to 'sell stuff,' I'll finally be using my comedy skills . . . for good instead of evil."

The show put together a team of writers to explore what the show would become. There were seven of us: Thad Mumford, Jeremy Stevens, John Boni, Jim Thurman, Tom Dunsmuir, Elaine Laron, and me.

Some of these writers had written for ad agencies, and others had worked for comedians. Elaine Laron, for example, had been a writer for a greeting card company. They were young and fairly new at writing a TV show. At age forty-three, I was likely the oldest.

We had about six weeks to come up with a concept and a kind of road map for the first season. There was no format, no title, no actors, just the idea. We were told we could write anything as long as it would encourage kids to learn to read. We were told we . . . "could not use the Muppets."

What? I thought, *No Muppets? That would have made the job sooo much easier.* But not using the Muppets had a purpose. Our young viewers might think, "Oh that's just more *Sesame Street.* That's for babies, like my little brother." So, our show needed to look and sound completely different. The music would be more electronic, and our scenery and graphics would have their own special look.

First, we had to be prepared for the task. We were given a crash course from reading experts. We found that there were a number of different methods for teaching reading. We would use them all: phonics, sight-words, the whole word method, and so on . . . an eclectic approach.

~

For a week or two we met with these experts. At one meeting they had passed out information on the ways whereby children learn to read. They spoke of a moment when a kid "gets it," when he sees how the sound of letters become a word. Of course, these were academics and they were using words I'd never heard to describe that moment. Words like "encode" and "decode." In the margin of one of the handouts we'd been given, I wrote: "Fargo North-Decoder" just to amuse Jim Thurman, one of our funnier writers (he lived in the suburbs and had a pet pig named Hitler). Jim thought it was a funny idea and mentioned "Fargo North-Decoder" to our producers.

I was asked to write a sample of what Fargo would be like. We'd already learned that one aspect of our show would be to explain sentence structure and punctuation. I wanted Fargo to be a hapless word detective who knew less than most of the kids watching. I based him on Inspector Clouseau (played by Peter Sellers in the *Pink Panther* films). In my first attempt, I had one of our actors, playing a kid, bring a note to Fargo, which the kid couldn't read.

The note said, "Please come to my party." Fargo, rather stupidly, turns the words into individual cards, which he places on a magnetized blackboard . . . but not in the right order.

The scene continued this way:

Fargo: (*reading*) "my Please party to come. Hmm . . . that doesn't sound right."

He rearranges the cards and tries again.

Fargo: (*reading*) "come to Please my party. That's kinda strange too. I see that the word 'Please' starts with a big letter, a capital letter. That's gotta mean something!"
The Kid: "Maybe that's the first word."

Fargo rearranges the words again.

Fargo: (*reading*) "Please to come my party."

He's stumped.

Fargo: (cont.) "This is a tough one."
The Kid: "Could it be, 'Please come to my party.'"
Fargo: "That's it! The mystery is solved! I've done it again! Any time you have a problem with words come to me, Fargo North . . . Decoder!"

~

By this time, I knew that learning to read involved a lot of guessing. I thought it might be a good idea to allow the kids to discover letters, words, and ideas while the grown-up, the actor, only suggested things. A young person might then make an educated guess, and often be correct, giving him or her a sense of accomplishment. "Positive reinforcement" occurs when a teacher compliments a student on a successful try.

I realized my natural instinct for funny character names could help draw our viewers into the program. I thought the show should sound less like school and more like fun.

The producers loved Fargo North. They saw him as a recurring character that the kids might like since they could feel smarter than him and also learn something.

Of course, I knew that few of these kids would know there was a city called Fargo in North Dakota, but the humor of the little joke had another purpose.

Our experts told us there were a certain number of adults who were functionally illiterate, who for some reason or other had never learned to read. If we could construct our segments to amuse them, they might join their children, their grandchildren, nieces and nephews watching the show, and not only experience some adult humor but more importantly, they might learn the basics of reading along with the kids, saving them the embarrassment of ever going back to school as a grown-up. Over time I learned that older siblings began to watch the show as well, just for the jokes.

I added a new character called "Child Chef Julia Grownup" (based on TV chef Julia Child). The producers wanted to have a character who phoned the show to complain about words that didn't make sense. "Alright!" he'd yell. "You got your T-O, your T-O-O, and your T-W-O, and they all sound the same! Make up your mind!" He was played by the very funny Jimmy Boyd. Since he was a crank caller, I named him "J. Arthur Crank." Maybe one person in a thousand knew there was a famous British film producer named J. Arthur Rank, but so what? It's still a silly name for the character.

Another personality would be obsessed with reading, a reading junkie. I named him "Easy Reader" (after the movie *Easy Rider*). He would be dressed as a cool "hippie" type. Easy wasn't content with reading signs, newspapers, and books, he would read anything, the labels on your clothes, the name on your sneakers, the words on your wristwatch, your tattoos, and so on.

One idea I had for him was to have other characters from the show try to limit his obsession with print. They'd take him to the park to commune with nature. Easy, sitting on a bench, would look up at the sky and say . . . "Oh. Goodyear."

~

I had now created a cast of characters, a family of offbeat types to help us teach our lessons. The producers seemed to welcome everything I had dreamed up; I was promoted . . . and became head writer. In retrospect, I realized that I had been the perfect person for this job. My long experience in creating radio spots would be exactly like our segments. The radio spots were sixty seconds long, and the scenes for our TV show were also short (for kids' short span of attention). My commercials always tried to "hide the message in the humor," and I wanted to "hide the teaching" in our show by "using comedy." Everything seemed to dovetail just right.

One day at the office, a young woman stopped by my desk. She was an associate producer named Naomi Foner, who would later become a screenwriter and give us two future stars: her son, Jake Gyllenhaal, and her daughter, Maggie Gyllenhaal.

She said, "How about a soap opera for kids?" I said, "Okay, let me think about it." She might have meant a parody of a TV soap opera. I had hardly ever watched a soap opera on TV, but from childhood I knew about them from radio. One of them, *Love of Life*, was first on radio, then on TV. At the end of the show, the announcer would always say something like, "Tune in tomorrow, to learn the answers to these questions: Will Susan marry John? Will Walter go to prison? Will Angela tell Sam about the baby?" And then, in a mysterious tone, there would be this cliffhanger, "And what about . . . Edgar?" So, I decided to do a radio soap opera, on TV, with almost no movement, concentrating only on words. I called it "Love of Chair."

Picture a young boy sitting in a chair in an empty room. The announcer says, "The boy is sitting," giving the viewers two seconds to take in the image. Then the print appears: "The boy is sitting." The viewer has another two seconds to read it; some will, some won't. Then the announcer says, "See the boy sitting." Again, a pause, to take in the information, followed by the print. Then the announcer says, "Boy, is he sitting." And once again, the print, the pause, and then the voice: "The boy is sick of sitting."

I was trying to pattern the words after an age-old technique used in picture books to teach very young children reading using as few words as possible. The most well-known was, "See Spot. See Spot run. Run Spot run." Then our announcer would say, "Tune in tomorrow and learn the answers to these questions: Will the boy stand up? Will the *chair* stand up? Will *you* stand up? And what about . . . Naomi?" (A tip of the hat to Naomi Foner, who had suggested it all.)

Now it was time to cast our actors. Since our audience would be inner-city kids who may or may not attend school regularly, diversity was important. The producers had already found our two stars. Bill Cosby was, of course, a very successful comedian, who would certainly have a following among African American kids. And Rita Moreno, a well-known actress, singer, and dancer, would obviously appeal to Hispanic children. For the rest of the cast, we hired Skip Hinnant and Judy Graubart, both adults but with childlike qualities; the very funny Jimmy Boyd; Lee Chamberlin, a beautiful Black actress and former model; and Morgan Freeman (little did we know what a movie star he would become). We also hired the real announcer, Ken Roberts, from *Love of Life* to voice "Love of Chair."

The producers wanted to use the "Love of Chair" segments often. I was thinking that meant once a week. They asked if I could do a new one every day. That seemed impossible, since I would have to follow, exactly, the template I had created. I may have painted myself into a corner, but I liked the idea so much I said I'd do it. Little did I know that would mean 130 episodes of "Love of Chair" in the first season.

The first twenty of them were not that hard to come up with, but as time went on, I'd sweat it out doing every new one. I'd usually write at night, like homework. I'd be awake until one or two in the morning, describing nearly nothing happening to that poor kid.

I was up late one night because I had to finish my next "Love of Chair" segment, but I kept putting it off to watch reruns on TV. At midnight I turned off the set. By that time, I was really sleepy, and I thought, *I'll just eat something.* I went into the kitchen and opened the cabinet. There were a lot of cans there. I picked one up and mumbled to myself . . .

"Maybe a bowl of chili will give me a second wind."

I laughed out loud. It was a pretty good joke, but I had said it totally by accident.

My plan for "Love of Chair" was to keep the boy in his chair as long as possible. The tenth episode would become my favorite. We had attached a belt to the boy and the chair (out of sight), so when the chair fell forward, he went with it:

"The boy is sitting.
The boy is sitting on the chair.
The chair is falling over.
The chair is sitting on the boy."

Due to the "A-ha moment," when the light bulb appears over the heads of kids and they "get it," we started calling it "The Electric Show." Then Joe Raposo, who had written a great many songs for *Sesame Street*, wrote a theme song for us, calling the show *The Electric Company*. It was very catchy. Everyone seemed to like it.

> *We're gonna turn you on*
> *We're gonna give you the power*
> *To turn the darkest night*

> *Into the brightest day*
> *In a brand-new way*
> *The Electric Compa-nee!"*

I loved the song and the name, but I still wanted the concept of the electric light bulb from the title song to sort of bookend the show. I created a short final scene and called it "The Last Word."

The image would be a bare light bulb with a pull chain and a word below it, then a pause, allowing kids to try reading the word, followed by the voice-over saying it. Then a hand would enter the picture and turn off the light . . . and the show.

The first word I used was "Pull." Our producers wanted to use it at the end of every show and asked if I could come up with 130 of them. Like an idiot I said yes. Just as in "Love of Chair," I had created a monster. How could I ever do it? Well, I liked the challenge. Now, fifty years later I'm not sure how I did it every day, but I did. Among a few of my early choices were the words "Break" where the chain broke, "Shakey" where the hand shook, "Shock" when sparks flew, "Twins" with two hands, "Glove," "Watch," "Ring," and so on. I finally decided the show would be called *The Electric Company.*

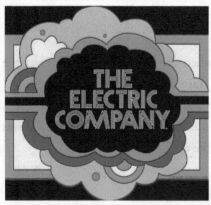

"The Electric Company" logo, 1971.
AUTHOR'S COLLECTION.

We reached out to animators to create short films for us. We got Mel Brooks to do a voice for one of them, animators John and Faith Hubley created several pieces for us, the great radio comedy team Bob Elliot and Ray Goulding joined us to voice a few animated bits, and Tom Lehrer, the popular and very funny songwriter and satirist, provided us with several musical numbers for animation. One of them was incredibly useful for teaching the concept of the silent "e." This rule of grammar was made perfectly clear in Tom Lehrer's lyrics:

> *An E on the end*
> *Can tell you a lot*
> *If it's there you say NOTE*
> *If it isn't, say NOT*

Working on the show seemed to help with some of the issues I'd been having with my ex-wife, since having a steady job in New York meant I wouldn't need to leave town now.

When the show premiered there was a lot of press, partly because of *Sesame Street*'s popularity. We made quite a splash! The producers had always been very appreciative of my ideas. Still, I was surprised when they asked me if I could also be a member of the cast. I told them, "Not if I continue writing; there wouldn't be enough time for both." Then they asked if I might direct the comedy sketches. Again, I had to decline.

I found that a lot of my time was spent writing "Love of Chair" and "The Last Word," a number of sketches for "Fargo North" and "Easy Reader," and editing the other writers' work.

Now that *The Electric Company* was on the air, I'd bring my kids to the office sometimes. They had been watching the show and had their favorite characters. Several times we visited the set of *Sesame Street*, where they met some of the Muppets.

Actor Frank Oz, who voiced many of the Muppet characters (most famously Miss Piggy), was a friend. When my kids and I arrived, Frank was holding Grover, another of his characters. The Muppet operators were normally hidden, out of sight, yet here was Grover moving and talking with Frank Oz standing right there. But Robin and Adam were so fascinated with Grover, they never once looked at Frank Oz.

Mr. Snuffleupagus, the giant elephantine Muppet, had been hoisted up near the ceiling to save space. The kids were confused . . . *What's he doing up there?*

We were coming to the end of the season. For the very last "Love of Chair," I came up with a switch for one of our best-remembered phrases. When the kids heard "And what about Naomi?" for the one hundred and thirtieth time, I wrote instead, "And what about . . . what's her name?"

~

After completing the first season of *The Electric Company*, I decided it was time to move on. As head writer, I had written or supervised 130 episodes of the show. *That's a lot of writing*, I thought. *Am I now just a writer?*

writ·er
/ˈrīdər/
noun
A person who writes books, stories, or articles.

That seemed to be true, because my very next job was as the head writer for a TV show starring Jerry Stiller and Anne Meara, a popular comedy team. I spent a complete season with them. Sometimes a little boy would come by the office . . . their son, Ben Stiller.

~

Over the past several years I had appeared in a number of plays, mostly Off-Broadway, mostly comedies: *Fallout*, *'Toinette*, and the cabaret revue *Twice Over Nightly* with Richard Libertini, MacIntyre Dixon, Jane

Alexander, and Mary Louise Wilson. It was at a club called Upstairs at the Downstairs, and we were asked to do several scenes from it on *The Ed Sullivan Show*.

The best of these Off- Broadway shows was *The White House Murder Case*, written by Jules Feiffer and directed by Alan Arkin. The cast was outstanding! There was a nucleus of actors, all Arkin's former partners from Second City, including Andrew Duncan, Tony Holland, J. J. Barry, and myself. Other actors included Peter Bonerz, Richard Libertini, Bob Balaban, and Paul Benedict.

The play was a dark comedy concerning the president and his cabinet at an emergency meeting on a Sunday morning.

There was a crisis in South America that needed immediate attention. Talk then turned to the First Lady, who had become a Liberal (God forbid), while her husband was an extreme Conservative. She was now an embarrassment to the administration. They worried, "What can we do about her?"

Act 2 finds the First Lady on a large conference table, quite dead (obviously murdered). The rest of the play deals with how to cover up the crime. It was, frankly, hilarious.

A couple years later, Jules Feiffer told me he had met a CIA operative at a party who had seen the play (this was before Watergate). He asked Jules, "How did you know what was going on behind the scenes in Washington?" Jules told him, "It was obvious."

~

An industrial film is made just for the employees of a given company for training purposes, or sometimes to act as a "pep talk."

In filming one of these, about selling properties in Florida, the actress playing my wife and I began to kid around to keep from being bored to death, trying to make each other laugh and also kind of flirting. Her name was Margery Bond. She was a feisty redhead with a good sense of humor.

We began going out now and then. Both of us were divorced and both lonely, so we cheered each other up. After a while she moved in with me. It was hardly a "committed" relationship. We were more like companions, but we got along well, and we were together for several years.

~

It had been quite a while since the divorce. Sarah and I were still not speaking, but I kept seeing the kids on a regular basis. Our agreement regarding visitation allowed me four weeks in the summer to have the kids with me, and then Sarah would have four weeks with them. This one year, in particular, seemed just the same. I told my agent I'd be unavailable for that time.

The kids and I had a great summer. Lots of swimming, playing games, watching TV, and going to the drive-in. We even made some home movies. One of them, a short melodrama . . .

> Robin is walking her doll in a baby carriage. Adam, a
> bad guy, dressed as a cowboy in a mask, grabs the doll
> and takes off. Robin chases him, begs him to return
> her baby. "No way!" says the kidnapper. She bribes
> him with chewing gum, and he hands over the baby
> . . . The End.

~

Then the kids joined their mom and left for Cape Cod, a place we'd gone to before on summer vacations. While they were there, I was surprised to receive postcards from the kids, which had probably been her idea. *She might be softening up,* I thought, *becoming a bit more civil with me.*

The evening after they were due back from vacation, I went to our house in Brooklyn to pick them up at the appointed time. I had been told not to knock, just to wait and the kids would come out. I waited, but the kids didn't show up. I knocked; there was no answer. I tried to look in the window, but the house was dark. Finally, I gave up and left. I thought, *Maybe their travel plans had changed.* I decided to try again the next day.

31
The Letter

The next day . . . the *very* next day there was a letter in my mailbox. I recognized my ex-wife's handwriting. We hadn't spoken in some time, so I wondered, *What could this be about? Maybe it would explain what happened last night.* Still, it seemed strange. I opened it.

I'm leaving. I'm taking the kids. We're not coming back.

I was stunned. I couldn't think. *Taking the kids?* It was insane! I thought, *This can't be happening. Surely she'll change her mind. Not coming back? How angry could she be?*

Immediately I went back to the house in Brooklyn, hoping against hope that they hadn't left yet, but knowing in my heart that they were gone. I knocked on the door again, this time quite loudly. No answer. I pounded on the door. Nothing. I no longer had a key. I spoke with the neighbors. They told me they thought the family was still on vacation but that the house had been sold.

For a week, I walked around in a fog with an empty feeling in the pit of my stomach. I called her family. Nobody seemed to know where they were, but if I had expected some empathy from them, there would be none. Instead, being her family, they blamed me for everything. In desperation, I hired private detectives to help me find them. I went to court, explained what had happened, and I was granted custody, which was, of course, meaningless; there was no one to have custody *of.* My kids were gone . . . maybe for good.

I thought about them every day. About Robin. About Adam. Nights of course were the worst; many times I cried myself to sleep. I felt helpless, hopeless.

At that time in New York there was a public service announcement on TV.

> *"It's ten o'clock. Do you know where your children are?"*

Every time I heard that it was like a knife in my heart. Two weeks passed. The detectives reported that, so far, they had found out nothing but would keep looking. They told me the family's disappearance had been carefully planned. She had left no forwarding address. I thought, *What about those postcards? Were those just to throw me off the track?*

My imagination was running wild. I thought, *What happens if they get sick? Or one of them . . . dies? Would I ever know?* In my mind, I had already thought of this as . . . two little deaths. *Oh my God! I've got to stop thinking like this!*

The whole thing was surreal. I now understood what it meant to be in a state of shock. Over the next month I kept to myself what had happened. I couldn't talk about it to my friends, not even to my family. Although I didn't think I had caused this, I still had a feeling of shame, like I was being punished. . . . But what was my crime? One thing I knew for sure was that when my kids went missing, a part of me went missing too. If Sarah's plan was to erase me from my children's minds . . . she would never erase them from mine.

Sometimes, lying in bed trying to sleep, I'd think I heard voices in the other room . . . *their* voices, but of course, I was alone. I developed a ritual; each night, when I felt near sleep, I'd whisper, "Goodnight Robin. Goodnight Adam." Saying it seemed to help.

During the next few months, I turned down auditions, sometimes even jobs. I was still having trouble sleeping and couldn't stop obsessing about them. I began taking sleeping pills. Still, I'd wake up at two in the morning with a start, feeling something was wrong . . . then remember what it was, and whenever I heard something on TV about "missing children," it sadly reminded me of my own story.

When not grieving over my kids, I began to wonder how Sarah had come to feel so desperate she had to leave town . . . was there something I had done . . . or not done . . . that might have driven her away? I was always struggling with the question: Why? Looking back, it occurred to me that the year I spent in *The Odd Couple* and the earlier year with Second City and also "Adaptation," that being alone all those evenings was probably hard on Sarah. Being the wife of an actor was likely not always great. Still, she never asked me to leave those shows.

At that time there was no such thing as a support group with others in the same situation as me. I was on my own. I had gone back to Dr. Kaplowitz, who told me about the many stages of grief. Among them were denial, anger, depression, and finally acceptance. I'd already gone through some of those but would have to wait for acceptance.

The detectives kept looking.

~

Dr. K suggested that the antidote to feeling depressed might be to keep busy; working and being around other people could help with that. I started going to every audition that came along. One of them was for a TV commercial for Salada Tea. I was videotaped on camera, talking about the many ways you could have tea. As I listed them, someone off camera tossed a lot of boxes and packages at me, the idea being how hard it would be for me to handle all of them. I'd receive some of them upside down or backwards, and as I spoke I had to juggle them around to their correct position so the labels could be read. The character was a bumbling spokesman (kind of like the "Fab" salesman).

At the end of all this, to show how hard it had been, I said, "Whew! I sure could use a glass of this stuff now." The idea was, in the actual commercial, they would throw a full glass of tea at me. Freeze-frame . . . and done.

The agent called to say I got the job. I asked her for the start date and when I needed to be there, and she said, "One o'clock." I said, "One o'clock? I've done a ton of commercials and the start time was always at seven or eight in the morning." She said, "I know, but that's what they told me."

When I got to the studio at 1:00 p.m., I saw my friend Alan Alda in the dressing room.

"Hi Alan, what's up?"
"I just finished doing a Salada Tea commercial."
"Oh, I'm doing one too. What was yours about?"
"Oh . . . they threw a lot of boxes at me . . . it was crazy."

We figured out what had happened. They liked both of us at the auditions and decided to film the two of us before choosing who they liked best.

It turns out, they picked me. So I got the Salada Tea commercial, and Alan got *M*A*S*H* . . . but, I'm not bitter.

When the commercial ran on TV, it was very popular and ran a long time. It was the funniest on-camera commercial I'd ever done. I won a prize, the Clio Award, as "Best Spokesman of the Year."*

~

In 1976 the ad agencies wanted to take advantage of the bicentennial in their commercials. Andrew and I were inundated with requests for humorous radio spots with a colonial twist. We used George Washington, Benjamin Franklin, Benedict Arnold, that whole gang.

Andrew, Lynne, and I considered writing a short play with scenes from colonial times in 1776. It was never produced, but here's one of our favorite scenes.

---

* That commercial for Salada Tea can be found on www.pauldooleyactor.com.

Betsy Ross is in her shop sewing. A group of Patriots come to see her.

"Good morning! We have just finished signing the Declaration of
Independence. We're calling our new country . . . the United
States of America, and we're going to need a flag . . . and you,
Betsy Ross, will have the honor of making it."

Betsy: "Take a number."

"Can you help us design the flag?"

Betsy: "I guess so, what colors do you want?"

"We're not sure, do you have any ideas?"

Betsy: "Well, I've got a box of remnants here, let me see, here's red
. . . white . . . and pumpkin?"

"This may be crazy, but how about red, white, and . . . blue?"

Betsy: "Whatever."

"We'd also like thirteen stars and thirteen stripes. When can we
have it?"

Betsy: "Uh . . . maybe in two weeks?"

"Oh, no! No! We can't wait that long. We'll be a country without
a flag."

Betsy: "Look, I have other clients. I'll be working all weekend. If I
fit you and your flag in, I'll be sewing stars and stripes forever."

"Alright. What about Monday?"

Betsy: "Oh . . . I'm not working Monday!"

"Why not?"

Betsy: "It's Flag Day!"

Then, Andrew and I were asked to do a tour of the major cities for
Time/Life magazines as if it were 1776. I was reluctant to leave New
York for all that time. What if the kids tried to reach me? It was unlikely,
but I still gave my neighbor a key to my apartment and my out-of-town
number, and he told me he would check the phone messages and the

mailbox and let me know if he heard anything. So . . . we toured the major cities in colonial costumes and powdered wigs.

Once the tour was finished, I returned to New York. My neighbor told me there had been no messages. My apartment always reminded me of my kids; they had played there, slept over there.

Finally, I took the framed pictures of the kids, the family albums, the toys and clothes they'd left behind, put them in a box and placed it on the top shelf in my closet . . . trying to remove reminders.

~

A year had gone by with still no word about them. I began to think, *What happens if I find them?* By law, I had custody. And yes, I could now get them back. But what would that really mean? Tearing them away from the only mother they'd ever known? Disrupting and traumatizing their lives . . . for a second time?

So I made a decision. The most difficult decision I would ever make. I told the detectives to stop looking. I decided that the best thing for my kids would be for me to step back and bide my time. I kept my same apartment and my same phone number. If they wanted to find me . . . they'd find me.

It seemed like there would be no closure. It was almost as if it had never happened.

32
Robert Altman

1977 was a big year for me. I was performing onstage in a comedy by cartoonist Jules Feiffer called *Hold Me*. It was a big success and ran for five months.

One night, the famous filmmaker Robert Altman saw the show. I was hired for his new movie, *A Wedding*. I would be playing the father of the bride, my friend Carol Burnett would be my wife, and Mia Farrow would play our daughter. I was excited! I would now have a leading role in my first film. So, after twenty-five years as a New York actor . . . *overnight* I was in the movies. I was forty-nine years old.

Robert Altman was called a "maverick," and he was certainly that. From the beginning, he rebelled against the "Hollywood Formula Film." Breaking all the rules, he marched to his own drummer.

I already knew a lot about him. I'd seen all his movies. His first big hit was *M.A.S.H.* After that came *McCabe and Mrs. Miller*, *The Long Goodbye*, *Thieves Like Us*, and a number of others. With each film his reputation grew. When *Nashville* opened it was a smash and made Altman one of the most important directors in Hollywood. I had learned that he encouraged his actors to experiment, to try things, even to improvise freely. Performers he liked working with would return again and again. I told a friend that if I didn't do something wrong on this film, I just might do more than one picture for Robert Altman.

The film would be shot in a mansion on Lake Michigan near Waukegan, Illinois, for two months. Margery came along with me. Altman liked her and gave her a small part in the film playing a security guard. Margery was thrilled.

Altman was known for creating a particular place inhabited by a lot of quirky, offbeat characters who came to life there. There was always a wonderful atmosphere on the set. It was like being in summer camp. He loved his actors, and they loved him. Everyone called him Bob. There were a lot of actors in *A Wedding*, about fifty in all, many of them stars.

There was Geraldine Chaplin, Carol Burnett, Mia Farrow, Dina Merrill, Vittorio Gassman, and many others. One of them was silent movie legend Lillian Gish, who was then appearing in her hundredth film. The stars, however, were never treated like stars; they were just actors like everyone else. We were one big happy family.

Bob invited everyone to the "dailies," the scenes from the film we'd shot the day before. These were festive occasions that allowed the actors to celebrate their work. My character's name was Snooks. He was an ignorant redneck type from Kentucky. His daughter was marrying into a rich family, and Snooks was pissed off about it.

I'd nearly always played comedic characters, never dramatic ones. I felt unsure about how I'd do this. But as I watched myself on the big screen during the dailies, I was pleasantly surprised. It seemed I *could* play a straight part just fine. I even began to enjoy my "serious" acting.

In the dailies I saw something else. There's an expression, "the camera loves her (or him)," that was certainly true of Lillian Gish; every move, every word was perfect. It was the same for the great Italian actor Vittorio Gassman; he never struck a false note. Of all those many actors, those two stood out.

We wrapped up *A Wedding*; it had been a great summer. We all exchanged phone numbers and now I felt a part of Robert Altman's film family (he was kinda like the father I never had). I also felt connected with his real family, his wife, Kathryn, his son Stephen (who worked as Property Master), and his son Bobby Jr. (who was on the camera crew). Margery also became close to the Altmans.

There were no messages from the kids.

A few months later, a friend of mine said, "Did you know there's a picture of you in *Variety*? You oughta check it out." *Variety* is the most well-known show business trade paper, read by everyone in films, TV, and theater. I picked up a copy, and there it was, a half-page ad:

ROBERT ALTMAN

announces his next film

A ROMANCE

starring PAUL DOOLEY

and MARTA HEFLIN

I couldn't believe it! How could I be starring in a film when he'd never said a word to me about it? I called his office and found out that we'd be filming in LA in a couple of months. Bob told me to bring Margery along; he had a part for her in the film as well. I was going to go from playing an ignorant redneck to starring in a romantic comedy, with my name above the title. He sent me the script. I was to be playing Alex Theodopoulos, part of a Greek family, in his fifties, still living at home, with a domineering father; a patriarch who treated his grown children like . . . well, children.

On an online dating site Alex meets Sheila, a much younger woman.

Altman had wanted to star Shelley Duvall and me in the new film, but Shelley was unavailable, so he chose Marta Heflin, who had played a bridesmaid in the movie *A Wedding*.

Sheila is a singer in a band with a domineering lead singer. I think domineering men seemed to be what they had in common. There were a lot of songs in the movie, and I liked the music. The movie's title, by the way, would change from *A Romance* to *A Perfect Couple*, since the leading couple were anything but. Every day I went to work energized and excited. I think it was mainly because I was the star of a movie for the first time in my life. I was grateful to Bob Altman for giving me the chance to play such an important role.

With Marta Heflin in *A Perfect Couple*, which we certainly were not. AUTHOR'S COLLECTION.

Bob had grown fond of Margery and gave her a very nice part playing my sister-in-law married to Dennis Franz, who played my brother.

Bob began thinking about his next movie and wanted Margery to star in it. He thought of calling it *Margie* or *Margo*.

For whatever reason, the film never came to pass (it's possible he couldn't raise the money), but for a brief moment, Margery was walking on air.

We finished the film. I called my neighbor in New York . . . nothing from the kids. Margery and I decided to stay in LA for a while.

33
The Big Bike Race

There was another film I was invited to audition for. I received the script and after reading about ten pages, I could see that the character, a father, was so much like my dad. I thought, *I could do this part in my sleep.*

I knew there was a terrific story there, and the part of the dad was a great one. At the appointed time I realized that this was not a normal audition; instead, it was a "table read" (that's where a script is read aloud by actors for an audience of mostly studio people).

This would be a wonderful opportunity for me. At a typical audition you're given three or four pages to read, but that night I would be reading every single scene in the entire script in front of a live audience of about twenty people.

As we began to read, I found I was getting all these laughs. *Hey!* I thought, *this is going great! How are they not gonna give it to me?* And sure enough, they did.

My son would be played by Dennis Christopher, who had also played my son in *A Wedding*. The other leading roles would be played by Dennis Quaid, Daniel Stern, and Jackie Earle Haley. Barbara Barrie was cast as my wife.

The original title of the film was *Bambino*. The studio later named it *Breaking Away.*

Margery returned to New York, and I went to Bloomington, Indiana (our location for the movie). When we started shooting, I noticed that the more we filmed the more I admired the writing. Steve Tesich had given a particular voice to every character and done it so beautifully that, with every word they spoke, we came to know them better. His humor for my character was so rich it was easy to find laughs. The script was simply . . . outstanding. No surprise that Tesich would go on to win the Oscar for Best Original Screenplay. It was the best part I'd ever had.

~

There was a scene in the movie that turned out to be the most emotional scene I had ever done. In the scene, my son, who loved biking, had just come home after having lost a race. Upset and in tears, he turns to his father for comfort. And since I was playing my father, who was this who needed a hug? It had to be *me*. I was giving *myself* the hug I *never got* from my own father . . . but I was *also me, embracing a young boy, who could be . . . my missing son.*

At the time, I remember thinking . . . *I wish my real missing son could see this scene.*

It turned out that Adam, still out of touch with me, had actually seen the film. Years later, he shared with me that watching that movie with his own father and an actor playing his son was just too much for him. He was in tears throughout the whole film, and when he saw me give that hug to my stand-in son . . . he had to leave the theater.

Hugging my movie son Dennis Christopher, the hardest scene I'd ever played. AUTHOR'S COLLECTION.

~

Time passed, quite a lot of time, in fact. My career was going well, but I was still trying to accept the possibility of never seeing my kids again. When not on location for a film, I would go back to therapy with Doctor Kaplowitz. We talked a lot about my lingering feelings of loss.

~

Bob's next film would be *Health*, a satire on the health food industry. He told me I would have a part in it but also asked me to help write the script. I told him, "I've never written a screenplay." He said, "Don't worry, you'll be fine." The man certainly had faith in me.

On location, in Florida, I met the cast: James Garner, Carol Burnett, Glenda Jackson, and Lauren Bacall. An impressive array of stars. As usual, Altman gave Margery a nifty role as a busybody. Talk show host Dick Cavett was there as well. He knew a lot about magic and taught me a few new tricks. Rather than playing a character in the film, Cavett was there to *play himself*. He told me, "They couldn't get their first choice." The film was not a success, but it was, as usual, a lot of fun.

~

Altman's agent, Sam Cohn, talked to me about becoming his client. He was the most important agent in New York. He had a star-studded client list, including Meryl Streep, Woody Allen, Paul Newman, Lily Tomlin, Robin Williams, Arthur Miller, Mike Nichols and Elaine May, Whoopi Goldberg, and many, many others.

Sam also represented Peter Yates, the director of *Breaking Away*, and Steve Tesich, who wrote it. Sam told me the advance word on *Breaking Away* was that it would be a hit and my performance was being extremely well received.

~

Breaking Away finally opened in New York, and I went to the premiere. The audience seemed to be enjoying it, there were lots of laughs, and the serious scenes were touching. But it was only when Dennis Christopher crossed the finish line in the big bike race that the crowd was on its feet, cheering and giving the film a standing ovation.

The reception of the film was a surprise to the studio, because, without any real advance publicity and a budget of only $2.5 million, it was not considered important. But once it opened, critics were calling it the "Sleeper Hit of the Year!" They loved the film! Character actors are rarely mentioned in reviews, even if they're pretty good (TV, magazines, and newspapers are more about the stars). At this point few people even knew my name. I accepted this as just a part of the business, but I began to wonder if this time I'd do better with the critics. After so many years, maybe I would no longer be: "also in the cast."

With this role, I did capture the attention of the critics. The comments I was getting for the film meant a lot to me. It felt like I was being rewarded, finally. I had never had reviews like this before. I'd like to share some of them with you.

"Paul Dooley has just created the performance of his lifetime, in *Breaking Away*. To see it is to know Dooley is certain to receive an Oscar nomination as best supporting actor. He is that good." —Gene Siskel. *Chicago Tribune*

"Dooley could win an Oscar for his role as the hilarious, harassed dad." —Roger Ebert. *Chicago Sun Times*

"He is the picture's comic heart, and he could just walk away with this year's Oscar for best supporting actor." —Stephen Farber. *New West*

"Dooley made his mark as a fine comic actor . . . he will certainly be nominated for a supporting Academy Award." —*The Tribune*. South Bend, Indiana.

"Dave's father . . . done with superb wit by Paul Dooley . . . deserves an Oscar nomination." —*Kingsport Tennessee Times*

"No one is as funny as Paul Dooley, and I hereby nominate him for an Oscar." —Roy Peter Clark. *St. Petersburg Times*

"Gives a superb . . . fabulous performance." —Janet Maslin. *New York Times*

"His portrayal is beautifully drawn and deserves high praise." —Gene Shalit. *The Today Show*

" . . . played with expert exasperation." —Richard Schickel. *Time*

" . . . played with delightful impatience." —Judith Martin. *Washington Post*

" . . . played with hilarious exasperation." —Rex Reed

" . . . played with comic grace." —AP. Hollywood

"Paul Dooley triumphs." —*Cue* magazine

" . . . outstandingly played." —*New York Daily News*

" . . . wonderfully played." —*Cosmopolitan*

" . . . brilliantly portrayed." —*San Jose Mercury*

" . . . a stupendous comic performance." —*After Dark* magazine

"It's worth a trip to the theater, just to see Dooley's double take." —*Variety*

P.S. I *did not* receive a nomination (although many people still think I did). As it happens, I won the D. W. Griffith Award for Best Supporting Actor.

It's been more than forty years and *Breaking Away* has become a kind of cult film . . . a minor classic. It plays frequently on cable, and there are many screenings of the film in retro theaters. The American Film Institute named it one of the top ten sports films of all time.

Personally, the movie has become my calling card . . . my signature film. I still get parts in movies, and on TV, because of it.

~

My father, now age sixty-nine, had a stroke that left him with an impaired left arm and a lame left leg. He no longer knew who he was, nor who anyone in the family was. There was, however, a surprising change in his personality. As you may remember, he was a withdrawn, repressed man.

Now he was always cheerful and always in a good mood. If my mother would take him breakfast in bed, he'd greet her by saying, "Hello, Sweetheart! How are you today?" He had no idea who she was; she was just grateful for the change.

On visits home I would sit next to his bed and say, "How are you feeling today?" He'd look at me and ask, "Who are you?" I would foolishly say, "I'm Paul . . . your son." He'd just turn away. I was devastated. It seemed I had lost my identity . . . again.

He would often wander around the house . . . *his* house . . . *the house he built with his own two hands*, and more than once I saw him running his fingers along a door frame, going over the corners where the wood was joined together. I realized . . . he didn't know *me* . . . but he knew *that door frame*, because he had *built it . . . his hands remembered.*

In *Breaking Away*, I based the father I played on my own dad. Walking with his son one evening, my character passed by the stone buildings on the college campus and talked about how, years before as a stonemason, he had helped build some of these buildings. They stop for a moment and he sits on a stone bench. As his son talks about college, in a nostalgic reverie, he runs his hand along that stone bench . . . *his hands remembering.*

~

I'm not sure if my father had even seen any of the films where I borrowed his persona as the model for my own. At age seventy-five, he died peacefully in his sleep. I was unable to attend the funeral.

I regretted never having told him how proud I was of him for all he had done for our family, and that despite his failings as a father, in my way, I loved him. He was a good man.

~

Sometime after my father's stroke, my mother had a real bathroom built in our house. Finally, she had a modern *convenience*. The *old* convenience, our outhouse, a familiar feature of my childhood, was demolished. I wish I had been there at the death of the outhouse . . . to say a few words.

34
I Would Gladly Pay You Tuesday

Altman's next movie would be *Popeye* . . . the musical! The cast would be stellar. Robin Williams would be "Popeye," Shelley Duvall was cast as "Olive Oyl," and Ray Walston as Popeye's father. I was to play "Wimpy," the hamburger lover, and Paul Smith played "Bluto" (the bad guy), and, of course, there was Baby Sweetpea.

Other actors would include Donovan Scott, Linda Hunt, Donald Moffat, Bill Irwin, and Roberta Maxwell, and Margery was cast as a Sweethaven housewife. Altman told me he was having trouble thinking of an actor who could play the part of Geezil, a pushcart vendor. I recommended Richard Libertini, and also McIntyre Dixon, who played Olive's father. They were both terrific!

There were also a gaggle of clowns, acrobats, and jugglers. Our cinematographer would be Giuseppe Rotunno (who had worked with Federico Fellini). The script, based on the old comic strip, was written by famous cartoonist Jules Feiffer with songs by songwriter Harry Nilsson.

Popeye would be filmed on Malta, a small country, actually a big island, in the Mediterranean Sea between Sicily and North Africa . . . the middle of nowhere.

Why Malta? I thought. Well, Altman had looked for a location in many places, including the coast of Mexico and Spain, then he heard that Malta had a tank where underwater scenes could be shot. He still wasn't sure which location to pick but while in Malta, he was having lunch at a pub and saw that the bathrooms were labeled "Popeye" and "Olive." He said, "That's a sign! We're shooting here!"

~

On the last day in December, 1979, I recall standing on a dock on New Year's Eve with Altman and a lot of actors drinking a toast to the New Year, the new film, and the imaginary town of Sweethaven, where our movie would take place.

Much earlier, Bob had chosen a scenic artist for *Popeye*, a designer who would create Sweethaven. That man, Wolf Kroeger, was a genius. Many months before, he had gone to Malta with a talented crew of builders who would bring Sweethaven to life. When he arrived, there was nothing there; it would all be built from scratch.

The town would sit at the edge of a beautiful blue-green bay and consist of fifteen or so buildings. There were no Hollywood "fake fronts." Just small houses with four walls, windows, and doors. There was also a large restaurant, the Rough House Cafe. There was even a church. The town was built with new lumber, then painted gray and distressed to look like a hundred-year-old whaling village.

In addition to the town, an entire cluster of buildings were put up nearby. There were offices, dressing rooms, makeup rooms, editing rooms, a commissary, a recording studio, and a rehearsal hall; it was like a whole Hollywood "backlot."

In the days before filming began, songs were prerecorded, we were given our costumes, and our makeups were created. In our rehearsal hall we had classes for singing, dancing, acrobatics, a class in Italian, an improvisation class, a juggling class, and even a Dixieland jazz band got started. We had our own community college.

When Bob first told me I'd be playing Wimpy, I wasn't even sure I'd be right for the part. I wasn't exactly fat and didn't have a big round nose, but once they put me in my fat suit, added my costume over it, gave me giant shoes, a tiny derby, and a silly mustache, I thought . . . *This looks pretty good!*

My one fear in playing Wimpy was that I'd be a fat man with a small mustache and a derby, and I did not want to look like the wonderful Oliver Hardy. I hope I pulled it off.

We worked twelve-hour days, had a quick dinner, went to see the dailies, and then slept. There was not much to do in Malta. We became our own small town and entertained each other. Our schedule was to be four months. As time went on, we forgot about Malta, forgot about America; we lived and breathed Sweethaven.

Here I was in a make-believe town, in a kind of make-believe country. Being there, and being so busy, allowed me to almost forget about my missing children. I'm sure it was a defense mechanism. While filming a scene with Robin Williams, Popeye tells Wimpy he has spent years *hoping to find* his father . . . just as I had spent years *hoping to find* my

Taking a break. (Left to right) Robin, me, and Donovan Scott, with Altman looking on. PHOTO BY PAUL RONALD

kids. Also, I realized that this Robin even had the same name as my Robin . . . it seemed the movie would not let me forget.

Through all of this, Robin was our court jester. We were fortunate to have someone so obsessed with being funny that the days went by quickly. Robin and I talked often about comedy and some of our favorites (we both loved Jonathan Winters).

Margery and I lived in a bungalow, and just next door were Donovan Scott and Carl Nakamura. Scotty played Olive Oyl's brother, Castor Oyl. He was a gifted comic actor and an outgoing, fun guy. Everybody liked him. Carl and Scotty were a gay couple and were free with hugs. Given my background, I was not a hugger, certainly not with guys. As time went on, I learned *how to hug men* from them . . . now I can't stop. Just kidding. We are still friends to this day.

Altman's grandson was chosen to be Sweetpea. When he arrived in Malta, he had developed Bell's palsy, a temporary paralysis that caused the baby to talk out of the corner of his mouth, making him look quite cartoon-like, and actually resembling the way Popeye spoke. After six weeks, the Bell's palsy went away and now Altman had to borrow close-ups of Sweetpea from earlier scenes to make everything match.

By the way, not only was Robin Williams great as Popeye, but Shelley Duvall was perfect as Olive Oyl. Shelley told me that in middle school they had actually called her Olive Oyl, so she was obviously "born to play the part."

With such a large cast and crew, and such a long shooting schedule . . . a lot happened. Babies were born, a couple broke up, a couple got married, then broke up, someone got fired, and someone fell down two stories and went to the hospital. At least twice a week it was somebody's birthday; we got sick of cake. After four months, most of the actors went back to the States, leaving behind the ten principals. From that point on, Olive's extended family was on a boat chasing another boat with Bluto, a kidnapped Olive, and Sweetpea.

That's when our schedule went to hell. We had hoped to finish our work on water in two weeks, but we'd shoot one day, then miss two days because of rain, then film two days and lose four days to high winds and choppy waves. Two weeks turned into two months. The budget went from fourteen to twenty million dollars. Paramount was going crazy; every day we lost cost them money. The studio saw the film as a money pit.

Finally, we wrapped it up and returned home.

~

The studio needed advance publicity for the film. Robin was back doing *Mork and Mindy*, and Shelley was in London, so it fell to Good 'Ole Wimpy to tour the major cities plugging Popeye in interviews for TV shows, radio shows, magazines, and newspapers.

I told every one of these journalists that hamburger-loving Wimpy was a part I played with relish . . . and also ketchup, and onions, and lettuce, and tomato . . .

~

Popeye opened to mixed reviews. Some were really bad, and others were just okay. Although in time the film made its money back, to Hollywood it was a failure. Still, it has since gained a real following with many fans, a lot of them children. 2020 was the fortieth anniversary of *Popeye*'s premiere. I did a number of interviews on radio and on Zoom talking about my memories of making the film. For me, *Popeye* was a once-in-a-lifetime experience, something I'll never forget.

~

The downside to being an actor in an Altman film was that the first half of any review was devoted to Bob's career and the movies he had made, analyzing many of them. The second part of the review told the story of the new film. In the end, there was little space in which to name the actors (although some stars would be mentioned). All the other actors, and there were always a great many of them, would be included under an all-purpose umbrella: "Also in the cast were a number of Altman's regulars." Not the kind of mention an actor is hoping for . . . but I still loved working with Bob Altman.

Out of the many reviews of *Popeye*, only one critic mentioned me.

> "The most extraordinary performance of all is rendered
> by Paul Dooley. How definitive a Wimpy is Dooley? He
> is Wimpy for all time, and Wimpy is now Dooley . . . his
> uncanny aptness is glorious to behold." —Andrew Sarris.
> *The Village Voice*

~

At the time I was living on the West Side of Manhattan. One evening, I was walking along 72nd Street on my way to Central Park and would soon be passing a legendary apartment building, home to a host of wealthy celebrities. When I arrived, there was a huge crowd in front of the Dakota . . . maybe a hundred people. They were crying, screaming, holding one another, or just staring into space.

December 8, 1980 . . . John Lennon had just been killed.

I milled around with the crowd, but before long, the tension was too much for me. I went home. An hour later I felt compelled to return to the scene. The crowd had increased tenfold. It seemed all of New York, and by now the whole world, was mourning the loss of a great and good man, beloved by all. I think the memory of that day lasted, easily, several years.

I had to wonder. *If I had walked by there just twenty minutes earlier . . . would I have seen it happen?*

It had been a while since my last film when I was offered a part in *Paternity*, starring Burt Reynolds. I had always enjoyed Burt's movies. His devil-may-care, good-ol'-boy personality was so enjoyable I thought I'd have fun. And I did.

One day, Burt invited me to his trailer to rehearse our lines for a scene. It was not exactly a trailer, but a custom-made, three-room apartment on wheels. A large bedroom, a large bathroom with a shower, a living room with a kitchenette, a giant television set, and he even had autographed pictures of famous actors on the wall; I remember Orson Welles and John Huston. It was quite impressive.

I found out later that the trailer wasn't provided by the studio for Burt . . . he actually owned it and rented it to Paramount. It seems a lot of stars were doing this. They could fix the trailer up any way they liked and then rent it to the studio. In the end, the actor still owned his trailer.

Once, I went to dinner with Burt and his then girlfriend, Sally Fields. We were having a delicious meal when his friend Charles Nelson Reilly came to the table to say hello (and to make us laugh, of course). Later, Burt ordered a bottle of wine to be sent to Charlie's table.

When the bill arrived, Burt was surprised to find it came to more than $300. He said, "That's a little high for three people." Sally looked at the bill. "Well, the wine you sent to Charlie cost $140." Burt said,

With Burt Reynolds in *Paternity*. More fun than a barrel of monkeys!

"Oh, right . . . do you have any money?" Sally laughed and started looking for her credit cards. I could only guess his wallet was in the car.

~

Because of my exposure in Altman's movies, and other films, I began to do more and more movies. In most of them, I'd be playing . . . guess what? . . . fathers. One father after the other, and after *Sixteen Candles*, I began to be referred to as Hollywood's "Movie Dad." I didn't mind playing all those parts. In a way, I think it kind of helped me . . . having all those imaginary daughters and sons on the screen.

Over a thirty-year span, these are the actors who were . . . All My Children:

Julia Roberts, Molly Ringwald, Toni Collette, Teri Hatcher, Mia Farrow, Helen Hunt, Robin Wright, Christina Applegate, Hilary Swank, Molly Shannon, Lea Thompson, Cheryl Hines, Bess Armstrong, Gina Torres, Valerie Perrine, Nancy McKeon, Sean Young, Philip Seymour Hoffman, Dennis Christopher, Jerry Van Dyke, Jon Cryer, and Brian Benben.

Could that explain . . . Movie Dad?

Since my real children were missing, all these Dad roles seemed strange. I began to wonder, *What is it about me that creates the impression that I am so fatherly? Had losing my kids, missing them . . . yearning for them, changed me in some way, become* so much a part of me *that it could* actually be felt *by an audience? Maybe.*

I could appreciate the irony of it all when a film critic, writing about my performance as yet another understanding dad in *Sixteen Candles*, actually wrote in his review . . .

"I don't know if there are any little Dooley's out there, but
if there are, they've sure got a terrific dad."

More than any other movie, my "late night talk" with Molly Ringwald is the best-remembered Dad of them all. Hundreds of young
women have written to me, or stopped me on the street, saying, "I wish
you were *my dad.*"

35
Molly and Me

I had originally turned down the offer to do *Sixteen Candles*. My new agent thought the part was too small; the parents of the young girl only appeared in the first and last five minutes of the film. He said, "With those great reviews from *Breaking Away*, I'm sure you'll be offered something better." They came back with an offer of more money. Again, we turned it down, and that seemed to be the end of it.

A month later, I got a call from John Hughes, the writer/director of the film. He told me he was a big fan of mine, had loved *Breaking Away*, and was sending me a new scene for the film, hoping it would change my mind.

I read the new scene and liked it a lot. It showed a more caring, tender side of the Dad character. In other parts of the film, he had been a distracted, kind of lame parent. I told John I'd do it.

I was pretty sure it would be a successful movie, but really just for kids. I spent only a week or two doing the film and became friends with a wonderful actor, Gedde Watanabe, who played Long Duk Dong. I thought Molly Ringwald was wonderful and young Anthony Michael Hall was terrific. Another young actor named John Cusack, and his sister, Joan, were also in the film. As I watched John, I thought, *This kid could be a star.*

I was waiting to film my new big scene and had lunch one day with Molly's mom. She was worried about the scene. Near the end of their talk, the script had the dad giving a friendly pat on his daughter's behind while saying, "Where the heck are your panties?" That moment bothered me too. A pat on the behind? If you can detect missing panties, that's more like copping a feel.

Molly's mom asked me what could be done. I improvised another possible version. I would have the dad say, "When you finally meet *your* Mr. Right, make sure he knows you wear the pants in the family." It's an innocent remark, but Molly is shocked, knowing she had loaned Farmer Ted her panties. Molly's mom loved it. We took it to John Hughes, who liked it too. That became the ending to the scene.

Once I had a day off from filming. I was in my hotel and got a phone call: "Is this Paul Dooley?" It sounded like Dustin Hoffman . . . it *was* Dustin Hoffman! I had never met him. He said, "I'm going to do *Death of a Salesman* playing Willy Loman. We'll tour with it out of town until it's in good shape and then take it to Broadway. I'd like you to play Willy's neighbor Charlie." I was thrilled! What a wonderful opportunity. I hesitated and then said, "Dustin, nothing could make me happier. I love the play, but I have a contract to do a picture with Robert Altman." I thanked him, he told me he understood, and that was it. I could have asked Altman to let me out of his movie, but this was my fifth film with him. He had gotten me started in films, and I felt I owed him some loyalty.

Here's my backstory with that play. When I was in college, *Salesman* opened on Broadway. It was such a huge hit that Arthur Miller instantly became the most important playwright in America and possibly even the world. He would go on to win the Pulitzer Prize for Drama.

Shortly after this, an LP record of the play came out. I played it over and over and over. I was not, then, able to appreciate all the drama and the poetry in it, but the theme, the father/son dynamic, the way in which Willy failed his son Biff could bring me to tears then, and now. Somehow, it hit home. It's still my favorite play, so not doing it on Broadway with Dustin Hoffman was a very big disappointment.

~

I was in Phoenix filming *O.C. and Stiggs* with Altman. I got a call telling me that my mother was in the hospital. Altman gave me two days off but told me I needed to return for one last shot.

I flew back to my hometown and spent time with her. Her condition was serious. She had had a fall, there were broken bones, and she had had a concussion. Her prognosis was not positive; she was seventy-nine.

Back on the set, the last shot of the film involved my character jumping from a helicopter into a man-made lake in a theme park (don't ask). Altman said, "One camera will be a wide shot, another camera will be a close-up with a long lens so we'll know it's you." The jump would be ten feet above the water. He said, "If it's a problem I'll use a stunt double, but I prefer you to do the jump." I agreed because I wanted to please him; Bob was like a father figure and he needed something from me.

Just an hour before the jump, I called the hospital and learned that my mother had died.

As I stood in the open doorway of the plane, ready to jump but concentrating on my loss, I thought, *What the hell am I doing here? My mother just died, and like an idiot, I'm going to jump out of a helicopter. This is not acting . . . just a stupid moment in a stupid movie.* I went through it like a robot . . . thinking about her.

She had been the emotional heart of our family. She would laugh with us, give us hugs, and just "be there" for us. She would actually dance around the room in moments of abandon and sing on our front porch swing, always trying to overcome the misery of my dad. More than ever, I now knew how much I loved her.

Her passing made me recall that after *Popeye* opened, I had gone back home to see her. I took with me a souvenir, a sort of plush pillow shaped like Wimpy. She seemed to love it. For the next few years, she would sit in her easy chair, and just across, in his *own* easy chair, was this replica of me in costume and makeup. When the end came, she had asked that her own private Wimpy be buried with her, a somewhat surprising . . . yet still touching request. We honored it.

~

I returned home for her funeral. Later, I was sorting through her belongings and came across a photograph I had never seen before. The family didn't own a camera, so there were very few pictures. This one took me by surprise. I talked to my aunt about it. She explained that, during World War II, my mother had taken a job.

There was a small airport near where we lived; not an actual airline, just a place to take flying lessons. It had been converted to a training center by the Army for men learning to fly. My mother had been hired as a cook and a baker for their commissary. She worked only four hours a day preparing lunch while we kids were in school. Other local women prepared other meals. I really never knew about it. She may not have even told Dad.

Every day, she would come into contact with about forty young men away from home (my mother was about forty at the time, and, as I mentioned, she was good-looking). I'm sure a little flirtation was going on. She got a lot of attention, and I'll bet she got a lot of compliments on her meals (something my mother had never heard at home). She also baked cakes and pies for these young men. I don't know if she worked there for a few months or a few years.

The photograph is remarkable. It was a window into a new version of my mother. I could see in her face the pride she was feeling, the sense of being needed and appreciated, having her moment in the sun. I still have that photo . . . and treasure it.

~

A few years later I was contacted by a lady from the Smithsonian Institute.

"Is this Paul Dooley?"
"Yes, it is."

"We've heard you know a lot about vaudeville."

"Well, yeah . . . quite a bit."

"We're planning to do a vaudeville show, live, at our theater here in Washington, DC. Do you have any written material?"

"Well, no. Not exactly. Everything I know is just in my head."

"Well, if you'd like to join us, just come to Washington the first week in June . . . and bring your head with you."

I laughed and said, "I'll be there!"

Later, she called to ask if I could direct the comedy sketches. I told her, "I would love to." Later still, she asked if I could help find the actors. I said, "Lady, look no further."

I thought this could be a lot of fun. I could pick the material and cast myself in the show.

There was a comedy team in vaudeville, two Jewish fellas, Smith and Dale, who had been together more than fifty years. The act was called "Dr. Kronkheit and His Only Living Patient." The play, and the movie *The Sunshine Boys*, by Neil Simon, is based on their act.

I had seen them many times on *The Ed Sullivan Show*, doing the doctor sketch. In the 1960s, vaudeville was revived on Broadway at the Palace Theatre with Judy Garland headlining and Smith and Dale as her opening act. I was finally going to see them . . . in person. I went to the show four times, and by the end I had memorized their act.

For the Smithsonian show, I decided to do the "Dr. Kronkheit" sketch. I asked a friend of mine, Joe Silver (I knew he also loved Smith and Dale) to play the patient, and I would play the doctor. Both characters used very heavy Jewish accents. Here's a sample of their routine.

If you're a doctor, where did you practice?

In Cairo I practiced.

Oh, you're a Cairo Practicer! What prices do you charge?

It's ten dollars for the first visit . . . and five dollars for the second visit.

Well . . . here I am again!

You cheapskate! Get out!

I'm going . . . I bet you don't even have a license.

Of course I do! What an insult! Get out! . . . *I'm losing my patience!*

I shouldn't even be here!

It was as close to vaudeville as I'd ever get.

~

Claudette Sutherland, an actress with whom I'd worked many times on radio, asked if I wanted to be a part of a workshop with a group of actors who'd meet once a week and improvise, just for fun. We'd all chip in a few bucks to rent a rehearsal room. I said, "Count me in!"

There were seven of us, mostly commercial actors, friends of mine, all older than fifty. I was the only one with improv experience, so I guided them a bit, but they were all good at comedy, and, honestly, improv is not that hard to learn. This went on for a couple of months, and then I had to leave to do a film called *Endangered Species*.

~

When I went back there was a new face in our workshop. It belonged to Winnie Holzman. She was an actress and a writer, and it was clear that she was a great addition to the group. She was, maybe, twenty-five years old.

I had met Winnie once before but only for a couple of hours. When I was writing for Stiller and Meara, one of the other writers, Don Perman, asked me if I would come to his apartment and listen to him and his friends perform a show they had written. They ran through their show, and it was very funny. The acting and the writing were both excellent, and I told them this. But, as just one person listening to them, I never laughed at all. Still, I hoped I had helped them. Their show would come to be called *Serious Bizness*.

The actors in our improv group had found that Winnie was naturally funny and a good improviser. I liked working with her and was impressed with her mind . . . and her sense of humor.

36
Blue-Green Eyes

Over the next few months, when we all went out to eat after the improv group met, I sometimes picked up Winnie's check. I knew she didn't have a lot of money, and I liked her. The two of us would also linger at the subway stop, talking. It took a while before I realized I was actually attracted to her (and not just to her mind). Our age difference might have made a romance unlikely; I was easily twenty-five years older than her.

One of the first things I noticed about Winnie were her eyes. They were blue-green with a hint of hazel. I found them warm, inviting . . . even enticing. I can't say what, if anything, she thought of my eyes. I'll have to wait for *her* book to find out.

Winnie was, in a word, lovable (I know I sound like a press agent, but for me, it's true).

She was, and is, the nicest person I had ever met.

Oh, no! I've gotta call Alan Alda and explain . . . he's gonna be devastated.

~

Winnie and her comedy group, Serious Bizness, were now performing in comedy clubs and theaters in New York. They were both actors *and* writers. The company included Winnie, David Babcock, Don Perman, and Jenny Allen. They even once appeared on the *David Letterman Show*.

~

By this time, my own improv group had improvised enough scenes that we had a story and a cast of characters. The plan was to show our idea to a producer who might help us sell it as a TV sitcom.

A meeting was set up at his penthouse. I arrived early and got on the elevator, and there was Winnie. She looked different, more dressed up, and with makeup on. I said, "You look nice." She blushed and said, "Thanks. It's for the, you know, the . . . meeting, and also, it's my birthday." I said, "Happy Birthday." She said, "Thanks. I have something for you!" and she gave me a tiny jokebook from a Cracker Jack box. I looked at her, and on an impulse, I kissed her; but I mean . . . I really kissed her . . . for the first time.

As the meeting ended, I asked if I could drive her home; she lived all the way uptown in Washington Heights, near the George Washington Bridge. At her apartment house I stopped and said, "Why don't you go on up. I'll find a parking place and then I'll come up." She looked at me, surprised, and said, "You can't come up. I'm living with someone." Now the surprise was on me. I had no idea, but she already knew I was living with someone.

Since our group met once a week, Winnie and I continued to see each other. We were certainly infatuated but tried not to show it to our fellow actors . . . of course they could tell anyway. We both wanted our relationship to be out in the open, but since we were both living with other people it was complicated. For several months we found time to be together. I think we were falling in love but were afraid to admit it to ourselves.

One evening we were walking around Manhattan; it was winter, and a light snow was falling. There were Christmas lights everywhere, and it was a romantic setting. I decided to open up and tell Winnie about the situation with my kids. That moment seemed to change everything. I had now trusted her enough to share my secret with her, and she felt even closer to me than before. We felt free, finally, to say I love you.

Winnie Holzman. She had beautiful eyes, and I only had eyes for her.
AUTHOR'S COLLECTION.

We were standing in front of the famous Waldorf Astoria hotel. I mentioned to her that I had spent one night filming there in *The Out of Towners* with Jack Lemmon. Within an hour she walked into her apartment, idly turned on her TV, and saw a film clip of me . . . with Jack Lemmon in *The Out of Towners*.

As I was writing about that time for this book, Winnie said that, when I told her about my missing kids, she felt that it was the missing piece of a puzzle. Before that, she knew that she was in love with me but sensed something unknowable about me, but now it all made sense. By knowing my pain, she finally knew me.

For the next few months, we would be together whenever we could. It was romantic, yet somehow forbidden. Finally, Winnie could no longer stand hiding the truth. She left her guy and moved into her own place. She asked me if I was going to end my relationship too. I said, "Yes," but couldn't tell her when. After a moment she said, "Well, as long as you're living with someone, I can't see you anymore. So, unless that changes. . . ."

~

This hit me hard. My feelings for Winnie were very strong, but my fondness for Margery, and our history together, made this a hard choice for me. Margery and I had now been together for several years, which made the idea of breaking up difficult.

About that time our improv group disbanded. There was no longer a need for Winnie and me to see each other.

A couple of months went by. I was very depressed. Margery couldn't help but notice. I kept thinking about Winnie and how much I missed her. I went to Toronto for a couple of months to film *Strange Brew* with Rick Moranis and Dave Thomas, from *SCTV*, and the great actor Max von Sydow.

While in Toronto, I was offered the part of the father in the film *A Christmas Story*, but I turned it down. I wanted to get back to New York and possibly see Winnie again. But once there, I didn't call her. Since I was still with Margery, I knew it wouldn't be fair.

Then one day, Margery said to me, "I'm moving. I'm going to live in LA." She didn't tell me why and I didn't ask. I suspect that she felt me pulling away from her . . . becoming more distant.

Margery had friends in LA from the Altman films, since she had played small parts in all of them. She'd stay with one of those friends until she got settled. The next morning, she was gone.

Of course, her decision was a godsend for me. Before I could break up with her, she broke up with me. My dilemma of choosing between two women was over.

~

I called Winnie to tell her the news. She was thrilled, and so was I. Now we could find out what our relationship was really going to be. For the next year we were together and very happy, each of us still living in our own apartment but now free to be together all we wanted to.

Winnie was getting more and more curious about my age. I have always looked about ten or fifteen years younger than I am. She went to the Lincoln Center Library and looked me up. When she found I was fifty-one, she had to sit down. *Oh my God*, she thought, *that is old!* . . . but despite that, I guess she still loved me.

37

The Phone Call

I was at home one afternoon when my phone rang.

"Hello?"
"Is this Paul Dooley?"
"Yes."
"Are you the actor?"
"Yes, I am."

It was a woman's voice.

"Your daughter . . ."

I could hardly speak.

"You mean . . . do you mean . . . Robin?"
"Your daughter . . . Robin, is working at the animal shelter in Madison, Wisconsin."
"Who . . . who is this?"
"I'd rather not say."
"Okay. That's fine. Thank you. Thank you so much."

She hung up.

Oh my God! The call I had been waiting for . . . for a *very, very long time*. To this day I don't know who that person was, but I will forever be grateful to her.

I found the number and reached my daughter at work. We had a short conversation, and she asked me to call her later. That night we spoke for ten minutes. It was unreal. She was a whole different person now, sounding much more grown up. She was reluctant to tell

My reunion with Robin in Chicago. AUTHOR'S COLLECTION.

me about all that had happened. I was careful not to say anything that might upset her. It was a very tentative conversation. I told her how happy I was to be speaking with her, how much I'd missed her, and, as I said goodbye, I told her, "I love you."

A week later we spoke again. She wasn't sure about seeing me. She was living with friends there, kind of on her own. The rest of the family had moved away.

Finally, I flew to Chicago to meet her. I was *overjoyed*. She was . . . *uncertain*, even sort of *wary*. It must have been very strange for her, meeting me like this. After all, she hadn't seen me for ten years.

There was still a bit of distance between us, but after a few more visits we weren't so far apart.

My reunion with Adam in New York. PHOTO BY BEGLEITER.COM

Soon after that visit, my son, Adam, called me. He had found my number in the New York phone book. I arranged to meet him at a hotel . . . on neutral ground, allowing him to have his own space. I did that because a reunion could have been traumatic for him. For me, it was more of a celebration. Within days he moved into my apartment. Our reunion was complete.

～

It was wonderful having him with me. He was eighteen now, but I sensed that, emotionally, he was still that young boy from years ago. I wasn't sure what he might have been told about me, but I guessed it was not that great. There was a lot that we didn't talk about.

I noticed a remarkable thing. He had a sense of humor that was, in an uncanny way, exactly like mine. I hadn't seen that before he disappeared, but he had come back . . . as another me, sharing my love of wordplay.

Was it nature or nurture? My guess is that, early on, one of the ways he bonded with me was the way my mind worked. Anyway, there were now two of us with the same instincts. We would often make the same joke at the same time, and, as a result, he was even more fun to be with.

It took time for him to get used to such a change in his life, and I felt he was doing well. However, years later, Adam shared with me that he had been terrified meeting with me. He must have considered the possibility that I might reject him; after all, he may have felt I'd abandoned him once before when I left home. He also told me this uncertainty was there for many, many months as we were trying to establish a new father/son relationship. At the time, I was not aware of all his feelings.

Adam had had an accident when he was age three, a serious head injury. A restaurant was found to be negligent. A settlement awarded him $8,000, which I'd put in a bank account at the time. With interest, it came to more than $12,000. Now that he was an adult, it was his money. I considered giving it to him in the form of an allowance of some sort and keeping the rest in the bank for him. But then I thought, *What the hell! He's a grown-up now.* He had just enrolled in New York University's Film School, and knowing he had money in the bank would allow him the luxury of focusing on his studies without any financial concerns.

I also wanted to reward him, to make up for everything he had missed out on, all that I'd not been able to give him.

~

When Adam finally met Winnie, he seemed to like her. Which was no surprise to me since I found her so likeable . . . well, lovable. He was heading for NYU's Film School, and they would soon have NYU in common.

New York University was about to offer an MFA in Writing for Musical Theater. A friend of Winnie's from college, Mitchell Ivers, told Winnie he was applying for it and urged her to apply also. Winnie was not sure it was right for her.

She had gone to Princeton, where she studied English Literature with a concentration in Poetry. Her friend Mitchell tried again, telling her that the program wanted to include more women. If she applied, she might get a scholarship. Winnie applied and sure enough, she got a scholarship. This was a decision that would change her life.

What an amazing opportunity it was for her. The program consisted of a series of seminars with Broadway professionals. There was Leonard Bernstein, the famous classical composer who wrote the music for *West Side Story*, Stephen Sondheim, who wrote the lyrics, and Arthur Laurents, who wrote the book (the book of a musical being the story and the dialogue). There were other successful Broadway names who came to share their know-how with the students: Adolph Green and Betty Comden, who had written many Broadway musicals, and Stephen Schwartz, who had created *Godspell* and *Pippin*. Stephen would later play a crucial role in Winnie's career.

To receive their master's degree, the students would have to write their own musical. There were composers, lyricists, and book writers among them. They all found partners to work with. Winnie wound up with David Evans. He would write the music, and she would do the lyrics. Her study of poetry would certainly come in handy.

Arthur Laurents took Winnie and David under his wing. They wrote a musical called *Birds of Paradise*. Once they graduated, Arthur continued helping them as a mentor. They would meet him from time to time, and he would give them notes on their work.

Winnie and David found a producer to mount their musical Off-Broadway. Arthur Laurents would direct *Birds of Paradise*. It was a wonderful show. I loved the songs, the story, and the actors, but the reviews were not positive . . . only the *New Yorker* liked it. It had a short run.

Winnie, Adam, and I were spending a lot of time together watching TV, going to the movies, playing card games. I was feeling really good about everything.

I still owned the country house and often Adam, Winnie, and I spent weekends there. Sometimes, Robin, now living in Connecticut, joined us. Both kids still had memories of that place. I started to feel like I had a family again.

~

I got a call from Anne Meara, from the team of Stiller and Meara, with whom I had worked on *Take Five* after *The Electric Company*. Anne knew Winnie, and she asked if the two of us could write some radio commercials for them. She and Jerry were extremely popular on radio commercials. She told me that recording these commercials took very little time, but writing them was much more demanding. So, for quite a while, Winnie and I provided the scripts for their radio spots.

~

Winnie was ready to get married but I had my doubts. I knew that I loved her but wondered, seriously, about my track record as a husband . . . two failed marriages, being unfaithful, and my age.

I knew I wouldn't marry me!

I also had my kids to think about. I needed to be there for them, to be responsible, to be, after all this time, the best father I could be. I shared with Winnie my misgivings and proposed a sort of test run. "I'll leave my apartment to Adam. We'll get our own place for a year. Then, if we don't hate each other, we'll get married." She signed on.

We were both enjoying living together, yet, despite our one-year agreement, after maybe three months, Winnie said, "C'mon. This is working! Let's get married!" I hesitated.

A month later she said, "My birthday's coming up. I want to be married before I'm thirty." The day before her birthday I gave her a card.

> Happy Birthday, Sweetheart!
> While you're still 29 . . .
> Will you be mine?
> I really love you. I'm ready now.
> Let's get married! Holy cow!!

We were married in New York at her parents' apartment with just her family and a few friends. Oh, and of course . . . a rabbi.

The reception was at the Player's Club, an actors' private club and formerly the home of the great actor Edwin Booth. There were ninety guests, and among them were my kids, Robin and Adam.

~

As I committed myself to Winnie, everything I had been working on in my therapy made sense. My other relationships with both my wives, and again with Margery, had avoided true commitment, which I've come to recognize as a fear of intimacy on my part. Because of that I had probably undermined those relationships. Now, I wholeheartedly embraced being a better partner for Winnie.

They say opposites attract. Maybe they're right. In temperament, my wife and I could not be more different. She's an extrovert, I'm an introvert. She's outgoing, I'm more stay-at-home. She can be impatient, I'm more like . . . an outpatient. She easily has a hundred friends, I have four . . . no, wait . . . three. She loves her friends and shares with them. When I'm with my three friends we share too . . . but mostly it's just jokes. She's like a sunny day, I'm like . . . cloudy with a chance of rain. Winnie is youthful . . . I am old, well, not just old . . . but old with an "e" . . . olde.

Saying that I have three friends is not really true. All of Winnie's friends have become my friends, as well. A great many of them are writers and actors, and I love them as much as she does.

~

I'd like to fast-forward twenty years to LA when Winnie and I renewed our vows. We were gathered at the church with, maybe, thirty friends . . . but the rabbi didn't show up. We waited fifteen minutes and then called him. "Where are you?" He thought it was for the next day. He promised he'd be there in thirty or forty minutes. *What?* Winnie began to panic. . . . "What are we going to do?" I said "Never mind him. We have our vows, we're actors, we *met* improvising . . . we can do it ourselves."

And so, we did.

It went beautifully. We both learned that this renewal ceremony was more heartfelt and more loving than our actual wedding. We didn't know each other nearly as well then as we did now. I recommend it to other couples.

Before we renewed those vows, I thought I knew everything about Winnie, but twenty years later, I truly understand who she is.

Winnie is the most loving, caring, supportive, generous person I've ever known.

38
A New Life

Winnie said she wanted a child. I was then fifty-five and worried that any child I had might be in high school when I, well . . . might be gone. Winnie said, "I know that's a possibility, but even when you're not here anymore, I want part of you to be left with me." What man could resist that? Within a short time, she was pregnant.

We started talking about names, and half the time it was just for laughs. If it was a girl, "Maybe Delilah Dooley?" "No, that's a stripper's name," Winnie said. "How about Tallulah Dooley?" "Not bad." I said, "Oh, I know! If it's a boy . . . Tarzan! . . . no? Okay. Wait! I've got it . . . Kareem Abdooley Jabbar."

Turns out she *was* a girl; we would name her Savannah.

Somewhat earlier I had been offered a role in a film, *Savannah Smiles*. I wasn't able to do it and recommended my friend Donovan Scott, who played the part, but I remembered that I liked the name . . . Savannah.

~

Savannah, baby's first headshot . . . ready for her close-up. AUTHOR'S COLLECTION.

We had not been married long when Winnie got a role in a one-act play Off-Broadway called *Raving*, by Paul Rudnick, a very funny playwright. The story involved three friends, just having seen a play and making fun of it. The actors were Sam McMurray, Winnie, and a third actor I was seeing for the first time . . . his name was Nathan Lane.

Both Winnie and Sam were very funny in the play, but Nathan Lane was in a class by himself. I thought I'd never seen a comic actor on the stage that gifted.

From that point on we kept in touch with Nathan and went anywhere he would be playing. One of the earliest plays was *She Stoops to Conquer* by Goldsmith. We went all the way to Brooklyn for that one.

Over the years we went to anything he did. After we moved to LA, we would time our visits in New York to see Nathan's latest play or musical, and he was as good in drama as he was in comedy.

There was a string of Off-Broadway successes in plays by Terrence McNally, followed by a lot of long-running hits on Broadway: *Guys & Dolls*, *A Funny Thing Happened on the Way to the Forum*, and *The Producers* (winning Tony Awards for the last two). We went to Chicago to see Nathan perform in Eugene O'Neill's classic four-hour play *The Iceman Cometh*, and back on Broadway, *The Front Page*, and one of his most recent triumphs, *Angels in America*, playing the infamous Roy Cohn. A chilling performance in an amazing play, and yet another Tony.

Nathan is so talented, and you'd never know it to meet him . . . he is so unlike the star he is. So modest, so soft spoken, especially backstage after a show (probably because he's exhausted).

I consider him the best stage actor Broadway has ever seen.

⁓

Jon Stone, the director of *Sesame Street*, asked me to join the Muppets in a special TV program filmed at the Museum of Natural History. In the story, the museum had closed for the day but the Muppets, and the human actors, had all been locked in. I played the guard who had to find them but always *just* missed them.

The program is a marvelous opportunity for young children to visit a famous museum and learn about art, history, sculpture, ancient artifacts, and more while being entertained by the Muppets.*

---

* The show is called *Please Don't Eat the Pictures*. If you'd like your kids to see it, look it up! You won't be sorry.

39
TV and Me . . . and Winnie, as Well

I went to LA to audition for a sitcom called *Coming of Age*. I liked film more than TV, but it was for a starring role. About a month later, back in New York, the call came; I got the job. I'd be needed in LA for ten days to shoot the pilot. Winnie and Savannah (who was now two) went with me.

In the pilot . . . I played a pilot (what a coincidence!). He had been forced, at age sixty, to retire from the airline and went kicking and screaming into a retirement home in Arizona. He hates the place, hates the people, hates the sun. His wife loves everything. His neighbors are so chipper they drive him crazy. They were played by two wonderful actors, Glynis Johns and Alan Young (who had starred on the TV show *Mr. Ed* . . . about a talking horse). Phyllis Newman played my wife, and comic Kevin Pollack was there, as well.

The cast got along well. Kevin Pollack, who was extremely funny, kept us laughing. We often had lunch together at the Universal commissary. One day, after we had all given our orders to the waitress, she turned to Kevin and asked, "And what would you like?" Kevin paused, then answered, "How is that *your* business?"

Once a TV pilot is completed, there's always a wait to see if the network likes it or not. Maybe a month later we got the "greenlight." Winnie and I rented a house close by Universal Studios, which was producing the series for CBS. We were given an order for four episodes. Barry Kemp was the showrunner, and he had an excellent team of writers, including Emily Marshall, who had written the pilot. After playing character parts for years, it was especially gratifying to be the star of a TV show.

Once on the air, the critics seemed to like the show. Encouraged by the reviews, CBS ordered four more episodes. Winnie and I went looking for a permanent home. We found one we liked, an English Tudor, also near Universal.

It was in a lovely neighborhood, a charming oasis of homes with abundant trees and flowers on walkable streets; quite a contrast from New York. Nearby, a business district of about ten blocks offered anything we'd ever need. We could walk to the bank, to the post office, see a doctor or a dentist, buy our groceries, and eat at any of a dozen restaurants; Italian, Chinese, Mexican, so much to choose from!

Still, I could not find a decent . . . potted meat sandwich.

Once in our new home, we began to invite family and friends to visit and stay with us. Winnie's mother came often to spend extended vacations. Sue was quite artistic. She was a painter and a sculptor, and she also created pottery. She made her home in Burlington, Vermont. Winnie's younger sister, Miriam, who also came for visits, has a home there as well. My daughter, Robin, who lived in Massachusetts, had since been married and would often join us with her son, Elias, for an annual visit. Friends from New York, actors and writers, would find a place to stay as well. We enjoyed being able to share a bit of sunny California with all of them.

We kept making episodes for *Coming of Age*. The actors felt we'd do a whole season, but after, maybe, fifteen episodes, without a word, we were canceled. Neither Universal nor CBS told us about it . . . we heard it on TV. That's show business! They love you when the ratings are good, but when the numbers start slipping . . . it's over!

Adam soon moved to LA. I was glad he was here; I had missed him. At first, he stayed with us, but then he found an apartment and sent for his girlfriend. Doreen and he had been together for a while in New York, and I was happy she would be joining him and that he'd have someone to share his life with. I also hoped that someday maybe Robin might move to LA, but she was still an East Coast girl.

Adam and Doreen were soon married. They had a son, Griffin, and Adam chose to be a househusband, hoping to be a fatherly presence for his son that he himself had missed out on for so many years. When his second son, Hudson, came along, he continued to be that same role model for him as well. I was pleased that they all lived close by.

Now I had my kids . . . and three grandsons. Not just a father, I was also a grandfather.

~

Margery and I continued to be friends. One day she said she'd like to meet Winnie and Savannah. I saw no reason not to, and Winnie was agreeable. Pretty soon we all became very close friends. Margery would attend our parties and holiday dinners, kind of like a part of the family. I felt good that we all had become that close.

Margery continued with Altman, appearing in the films *Short Cuts* and *The Player*, in which she had a pivotal role.

40
Ed and Marshall

Winnie's favorite TV show was *thirtysomething*. Visiting the set one day, she met one of the writers, Richard Kramer. He said, "My brother Jim tells me you're a good writer" (Jim Kramer knew Winnie's writing from her comedy group Serious Bizness). Richard asked her, "What are you going to do now that you're here?" Winnie said, "I'm not sure. I've got a two-year old, but I was thinking of looking for a writing job, maybe for film or TV." Richard told her if she wanted to write a few scenes, he'd take a look at them.

Instead of a few scenes, Winnie wrote a complete script, using all the *thirtysomething* characters. Richard generously read her script, and, even more generously, passed it on to the creators of the show, Ed Zwick and Marshall Herskovitz, who loved her writing and added her to their staff.

The "Cinderella" part of the story is that Winnie, who did not belong to the Writer's Guild West, and did not have a TV agent, had gone from little experience in writing for television in New York to landing a job on one of the best shows on TV. *thirtysomething* was known for its innovative writing, and many writers, with more experience, would have loved that job. Winnie's TV career was off to a great start!

~

Coming of Age was now history, but we decided to stay in LA for good. Winnie was now busy writing for *thirtysomething*, and I could actually get more work in LA than in New York.

Over the next few years, I appeared on the TV shows *The Golden Girls*, *Curb Your Enthusiasm*, and *Alf*, in the films *Runaway Bride*, with

Julia Roberts, and *Insomnia*, with Al Pacino, Robin Williams, and Hilary Swank, and in the musical *Hairspray*, with John Travolta, Queen Latifah, Christopher Walken, and a very young actress, Nikki Blonsky, who was really talented. My scenes were just with Michelle Pfeiffer, but John Travolta posed for a candid picture with me.

~

Savannah was watching a video recording of a segment on Sesame Street called "Learning about Letters," which she referred to as "Yearning about yetters." We all know how adorable it is when a little kid says something funny by accident.

Winnie was preparing dinner when Savannah asked if she could watch it again. Her mom rewound the tape, and after that viewing, Savannah asked to watch it once again. "Okay," said her mom, "but this will be the last time."

Savannah wanted to see "Yearning about yetters" again. Winnie, still busy with cooking, and annoyed with all the interruptions, said:

"No, Savannah. No. N-O. Yearn about those yetters."

~

Winnie and I read a lot of books to Savannah. On her own, she would leaf through those books herself. One day, Winnie and Savannah were in a restaurant, and the waitress left two menus. Savannah was kind of looking at one when Winnie said, "What would you like to eat?" Savannah said, "Muffin."

Winnie thought she was just remembering, but Savannah pointed to the word "Muffin." It turned out she had taught herself to read, at least muffin-wise . . . she was three years old. And she hadn't even *seen The Electric Company*!

We were amazed, but as I thought about it, I realized what must have happened. As we were reading books to her, she probably not only looked at the pictures but followed along looking carefully at the words, and after several readings of the same books she had put two and two together and figured it out. Winnie herself had started reading early and began to write stories at a young age.

~

I had not done a play for several years. Theater in LA couldn't compare with New York. Broadway theaters were clustered together, sometimes five or six in one block, and all of it contained within a ten-block radius. Very convenient.

In contrast, LA theaters were often miles apart. You would have to drive from thirty minutes to an hour to attend a play, or to act in one. Who would do that?

This is easily explainable. Manhattan is an island with millions of people, so space is limited. It's a vertical city that can only be built upwards. LA, also with millions of people, is a sprawling collection of towns spread out over five hundred square miles.

Also, because of the number of theaters in New York, the talent pool of stage actors is much larger there than in LA.

In 1992, I was offered a part in a play, a farce called *Lend Me a Tenor*, to be presented at the Pasadena Playhouse and directed by David Saint. I would be playing a somewhat hysterical manager of an opera house. I would be yelling (or screaming) through the entire play. As a result, I'd often find myself hoarse at the end of the evening. Drinking hot tea backstage helped; I also drank tea at home constantly.

In 1997, I returned to the Pasadena Playhouse for *After-Play*, again directed by David Saint, and written by my friend Anne Meara. The cast included the wonderful Marian Mercer and the equally wonderful Bea Arthur, playing my wife. It was great fun!

~

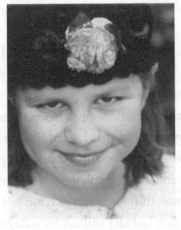

Savannah, age eight. We don't exactly look alike, but we certainly think alike. PHOTO BY ADAM DOOLEY

When Savannah was about seven years old, something told me she had picked up on my proclivity for wordplay. We were walking past a video rental place called Odyssey Video. She asked if she could get a video. Since there wasn't time I said, "Not today, honey." After a pause she said, "But Dad . . . I *oughta see* a video." I was very proud! A three-syllable joke.

~

When a new family moves into our neighborhood, sometimes my wife will say, "You know, we should . . . *have them over*." I tell her, "Yeah, let's do that."

For me, there are a couple of families I don't think I'd *ever have over*.

The Doldrums? . . . They sound kinda boring.

The Shenanigans? . . . I don't think so . . . Could be a lotta trouble.

~

I was surprised to be asked to do *Star Trek: Deep Space Nine*. The character was Enabran Tain, a Cardassian who had gained notoriety as the leader of the Obsidian Order, the secret police, of which he maintained control. He was married and the father of Elim Garak, a fact he never admitted publicly.

The fleet, under the command of Tain and Romulan colonel Lovok, aims to destroy the Homeworld. He offers Garak the opportunity to return from exile. He was a real bastard but fun to play.

The makeup was quite elaborate, with six or eight pieces of latex on my face, including a thing on my forehead that looked like a kitchen spoon holder. Also, two elongated, spine-like appendages going from both ears down to my shoulders, and a wig. Applying the makeup was a four-hour transformation and took thirty minutes to remove. I think I did only three or four episodes, but Trekkies still ask for autographs.

41
Claire

Sometime after *thirtysomething* ended, Winnie's mentors, Ed Zwick and Marshall Herskovitz, reached out to her. They were thinking about a new TV series about a young girl in high school. They wanted it to be unlike any other TV show about teens—something more real, more personal, more honest.

Winnie wrote the pilot. Ed and Marshall were pleased with it. ABC gave it the green light. Winnie titled it . . . *My So-Called Life.* They began looking for actors. They had seen only one other girl for the part of Angela when they met Claire Danes, all of thirteen when she auditioned. Once they met Claire the search was over. She was perfect! In the casting of the other kids, they also hit a home run. Jared Leto, Wilson Cruz, Devon Odessa, A. J. Langer, and Devon Gummersall were all excellent actors, as were Tom Irwin and Bess Armstrong as Angela's parents.

I went to a screening of the pilot, and I was blown away. All the supporting actors were wonderful . . . and Claire, well, what can you say? I was raving about her to my friends, "This girl is extraordinary. At fourteen, she has the talent, the poise, and the grace of a forty-year-old actress, and she will certainly become a star."

When the series went on the air, the reviews were excellent. Although it developed a cult following, after only nineteen episodes, the show was canceled. Again, it was about the ratings.

~

A TV show, already on the air, *Grace Under Fire*, starring female comic Brett Butler, held an audition for an actor to play her boss. The audition

consisted of a two-minute monologue, and it was very funny. I memorized it and aced the audition.

The new boss meets his employees for the first time and makes a
short speech. He is so phony, so insincere, that he'd say something nice
and then, reading from his notes, disinterested, he'd say, "Blah. Blah.
Blah." The entire speech was just a lot of BS.

His last comment was, "And remember, my door is always open."
Then he goes into his office, closes the door, pulls down the blind, and
we hear the door being locked. I did a lot of episodes over a couple of
seasons.

~

The call was from Christopher Guest. I greatly admired him because
of his work in *Spinal Tap*, the hilarious mockumentary starring Chris,
Michael McKean, and Harry Shearer. The three of them created fake
rock group Spinal Tap, complete with spot-on British accents, and
largely improvised. They had also written the songs for the film, which
is still considered a comedy classic.

Chris was planning a new film called *Waiting for Guffman*. He asked
me if I could come to Austin to film for just one day. I was anxious to
work with Chris since he was a comic genius. He told me I'd be playing a local man who, some years earlier, had been abducted by aliens
and kept on their spaceship for a while. I'd be improvising my scene.
As I left home that morning, my wife said to me, "Don't forget to get
probed!" (When people are abducted by aliens, they often refer to being
probed.)

On the set that afternoon I did my little scene, probably no more
than a minute long. Chris said, "Let's do one more take." I asked him,
"The same or different?" He said, "Whatever you want." I knew Chris
would like the character to sound like a "real person," so I hemmed
and hawed my way through it again, sounding like someone not used
to public speaking. I spoke of the many and diverse ways I had been

probed. Chris said, "Good! We're done! You can go home, if you want." So I flew there, did my scene, and flew home all in one day . . . never even had lunch.

When *Guffman* opened, I thought it was probably the funniest comedy I had ever seen. The story was about a group of amateur actors putting on a show. The cast was amazing. Chris had chosen the best actors to portray the worst actors. There was Catherine O'Hara and Eugene Levy (from SCTV), Fred Willard, Parker Posey, Bob Balaban, Lewis Arquette, Larry Miller, and Chris himself as director Corky St. Clair.

Next was *A Mighty Wind,* a kind of a musical with songs by Guest, McKean, and Shearer. I would be a member of the vocal group The New Main Street Singers. At my meeting with Chris he asked, "Do you play an instrument?" I said, "No, I don't." He said, "Can you carry a tune?" I said, "No, in fact I can *barely hum.*" He said, "Never mind. I still want you to be in it. You can hold a guitar and never play it. And, for the singing, you can mouth the words, no one will know the difference." And that's just what I did.

The only other picture I did with Chris was *For Your Consideration,* with all of his regular actors. What a privilege just to be along for the ride.

~

Another very funny fellow is Larry David. His show was a lot of fun because I was able to improvise the dialogue, just as I had with Christopher Guest. I played Larry's father-in-law and appeared in a number of episodes of *Curb Your Enthusiasm.*

42
Wicked

Wow! Winnie thought. *Stephen Schwartz wants to have lunch with me! What could this be about?* Stephen had created *Godspell*, *Pippin*, and many other shows on Broadway and had been one of her teachers at the NYU Musical Theater Program.

At lunch he asked her if she'd read a book called *Wicked*. She told him she *had* the book but had not yet read it. He went on to say he'd had a conversation with producer Marc Platt, at Universal Studios, who wanted to adapt the book into a movie musical. Stephen told him he knew the book but would prefer to do it first as a Broadway musical and then make a film of it.

Stephen had seen Winnie's early musical *Birds of Paradise* and thought they could work together on *Wicked* the musical. She was excited, and they agreed to create the show as partners.

The original book by Gregory Maguire was a four-hundred-page tome. It was a prequel to *The Wizard of Oz*, which imagined what happened before Dorothy got there. It was a dense, wide-ranging epic with many characters and innumerable story lines that, if followed faithfully, might become a ten-hour musical. They would have their work cut out for them.

Winnie wanted a place to write, away from the house, the phones, and the doorbell, so I designed a backyard office (14' × 14') for her. She calls it her "hut."

In the late 1990s, Winnie spent a few years off and on writing the musical *Wicked*, most of it in her new hut.

We had a pool in the back, about 40' × 20', and it was an oversized, boring rectangle that seemed to be too big for the yard. I decided to have it removed and designed a smaller, more intimate pool. The shape of it was a sort of figure-eight, with lots of curves . . . easy on the eyes. I added a jacuzzi on one side.

Ninety-five percent of pools seemed to have blue water. I didn't like the blue water. My new pool would have a pale green bottom and would appear like a pond you might find in nature somewhere in the woods.

Once the pool was finished, I built a path leading from our back porch to Winnie's hut. It curved around the jacuzzi, then curved again, and finally, curved for a third time and went to the door of her hut. I had the pathway paved, and she now had her very own . . . "Yellow Brick Road."

In the process, I had an aha moment. I realized, if I could draw a picture on paper, I could also create landscaping in 3-D. This newfound ability became a passion of mine.

~

I joined a group of friends to do some improvising at a club called The UpFront, located on "The Promenade," a pedestrian street with no traffic in Santa Monica, California, a few blocks from the ocean.

The improv company included Sevren Darden, Mina Kolb (from the original, original Second City), Ann Ryerson, Lewis Arquette, Anna Mathias, and a fellow with the unlikely name of "Beans" Morocco (and from time to time . . . the wonderful Richard Libertini). We were just a pickup team and had no idea how long we'd be doing it; we ended up doing it for five years. We didn't have a name. Sevren gave us one: The PostModernaires. We performed only once a week . . . on Saturday night.

We often started the show with just a handful of people in the audience, but since there was a huge glass window and passersby could see us doing "something" in there, by the end of the show we usually had a pretty good audience. We were never paid; we did it just for fun. I was available for 90 percent of the shows, but if any one of us couldn't be there for any reason we'd make a call and find another improviser. There was a huge family of improvisers in LA by this time.

It had been a while since I'd improvised in New York. Once I started working with this group, I realized how much I'd missed it and was glad to have a new outlet for getting laughs.

~

I appeared on *The Practice* about a dozen times, playing an eccentric judge. When you play a judge, you always say the same things: "Overruled." "Sustained." "Order in the court." "I'll see you in my chambers, Councilor." Pretty simple. Pretty boring.

In one episode, I did indeed see the lawyer in my chambers. We screamed and yelled at each other many, many times. I got an Emmy nomination . . . I guess for screaming and yelling.

On the series *Dream On*, I was a sixty-five-year-old man, just divorced, who is coming out to his son, telling him he's gay. The dialogue was so well written, so funny, and yet so touching. I received another Emmy nomination . . . I guess for being gay.

~

Winnie has a lot of friends. Many of them were from New York but now lived in LA, so, over time, we've all become very close, especially when they had children. It seems as if your friends' kids can feel like part of your own family; like we're now aunts and uncles.

Winnie's favorite cousin, Danny Stone, an actor, lives nearby with his wife, Rebecca, a former puppeteer and later editor in chief at Scholastic, Inc. Their daughter Annabeth and Savannah are close in age.

Breon Gorman knows Winnie from college. She and her husband, Tim Landfield, are both performers. They have two daughters: Miranda and Bianca.

Winnie met Robert Freedman at the NYU Musical Theatre Program in the 1980s. He is a screenwriter and a playwright. His wife, Jeannie Kauffman, is an actress and a singer, and their son is the multitalented Max.

Ron Fassler, an actor, and his wife, Margaret Nagle, a screenwriter, had two children, Jeremy and Charlotte.

We love all these kids as if they were our own.

~

Winnie and I are often asked to entertain at parties for friends. She, of course, is an actress as well as a writer and often comes up with killer lines.

Once, at a Thanksgiving party, we treated the guests as the original pilgrims. I told them what the meal would be:

"Wild turkey, cranberries, and yams. And plenty of sweets! Hasty pudding, pumpkin pie, oh, and a delicious apple brown betty . . . So save room for that!"

Then Winnie added . . .

"And after that we'll have a witch burning . . . so *save room for that!*"

At another party, in 2000 (it was the new millennium), I got an idea. I said to the crowd:

"Originally Robert and I had agreed to share the cost of this party. But then I thought, you know, Robert, why don't *you pay* . . . for this millennium party, and *I'll pay* . . . for the next one."

A joke I could use only every hundred years.

~

The play *Mornings at Seven* had originally been a hit on Broadway in the 1930s. A revival had also been done in New York recently, which was well received and was now closing.

The original company was coming to LA to do the play at the Ahmanson Theatre. The cast was a remarkable one, including Elizabeth Franz, Frances Sternhagen, Julie Hagerty, Piper Laurie, Buck Henry, Biff McGuire, and Stephen Tobolowsky. Very impressive.

Two of the actors in the New York company chose not to come to LA. Estelle Parsons was replaced here by my friend Mary Louise Wilson, and my other friend Bob Dishy's part was given to me. Our production here was a big success.

One night, backstage, as I waited to go on, I noticed Elizabeth Franz sitting nearby, and because I admired her and all the other actors so much, all extremely experienced and hugely talented, I began to think about actors and the acting profession in a fresh, new way.

Actors are, in general, friendly, warm, supportive, intelligent, honest, sensitive, empathetic, and usually have a good sense of humor. I thought, *What a wonderful profession to be a part of*!

Later that season, our company had won an award, Best Ensemble Cast. At the ceremony, a group of us went onstage to accept the award. Each of us said a few words of thanks. I found myself going to the mike and sharing my feelings of pride in all these actors.

I found myself choked up and close to tears.

~

For about four years, Winnie and Stephen had been working hard on *Wicked*. The two of them had shared many meetings, phone calls, discussions, and emails while finding ways to simplify the story and focus on just a few characters.

They did all this slowly but surely, since Winnie was also writing television, and Stephen was also creating songs for Disney animated movies.

They took the show to San Francisco for an out-of-town tryout. Through the rehearsal process Winnie and Stephen continued fine-tuning the show. Savannah and I were at home and we missed her. When the musical opened in 2003, the two of us went to see the show and to spend a few days with Winnie.

Now Stephen and Winnie were busier than ever, watching the show every night and rewriting every day. They were under a lot of pressure to *betterize* the script.

Sadly, Winnie told us we should go home since she had so little time for us. The musical, even though still a work in progress, was, to me, already brilliant!

The show closed in San Francisco, and the two of them reworked the script even more. It then opened on Halloween of 2003 on Broadway with Idina Menzel starring as Elphaba and Kristin Chenoweth as Glinda. Joel Grey played the Wizard, the late Carole Shelley (with whom I had worked in *The Odd Couple*) played Madame Morrible . . . and the rest is Broadway musical theater history.

~

When I first met Winnie, I thought her talent was as an actor, even though her improvisation revealed the writer in her. (Improvisation *is*, by the way, *writing*; otherwise, where do the words come from?)

But over time, my appreciation of her writing grew. First, when she created her early musical *Birds of Paradise*, and next with *My So-Called Life*. That groundbreaking TV series announced that here was a writing talent to be watched. The series still has a cult following. It was, however, even later on Broadway with Wicked, that her inventiveness with the story and the dialogue confirmed her reputation as one of the best writers around.

"What's so special about her writing?" you might ask. Well, in my opinion, what's special is this: She not only tells you what her characters are *saying* but what they're *not saying* . . . what they're *feeling*. This is referred to as "subtext." I'm aware that all the best writers write this way, but there are many writers who don't delve as deep into their characters, writing more on the surface.

Speaking of the writer's place in the theater, I'm reminded of something Marja Fear, my teacher at WVU, said in class one day that has stuck with me ever since. "In the theater, there is only one 'creative' person, the writer. Everyone else is an 'interpreter' of the writer's vision." Of course, those collaborators can make important, even crucial contributions to the play . . . the directors, the actors, costumers, set designers, lighting experts, or if it's a musical, the composer, the choreographer, and, of course, the orchestra.

But none of this would be possible without the writer.

~

Savannah's schooling was uneventful through middle school and the first year of high school, and then we learned about the Los Angeles County High School of the Arts (LACHSA), which offered regular classes but emphasized studies in art, music, and theater. We enrolled her there. That's where she blossomed, meeting a lot of other kids her age who had the same interests as her, which made her time there the best learning and growing experience ever.

Savannah headed off to college at Bennington, where she would major in writing. While there, a friend of Winnie's read some of Savannah's writing, which led to an assignment to write a script for a TV show. She was twenty-one years old and had her mother's writing ability. ABC family asked her to create a movie for TV based on a book called Huge. She began her work.

After graduation, her TV script grew from a movie for TV into a summer series on ABC Family. The program followed a group of teens at a weight-loss camp for the summer. The title . . . *HUGE.* Savannah would be producer and head writer for the series. Winnie decided to join her, and together they created a full season of ten episodes. I was very proud of them both.

~

Bob King, an actor and a friend of mine from my commercial days, was now living in LA. Winnie became close friends with his wife, Linda. We were invited to their summerhouse at Lake Arrowhead for a week-end. They had plenty of rooms, and the guests would be sleeping over. Another couple, Jim Karen, and his wife, Alba Francesca, would be there as well.

Casually, I began a conversation with Jim Karen and found him, and his stories, fascinating. He was my age and had been an actor for years on Broadway and in films. I had seen him many times. When he mentioned that he and Buster Keaton were friends . . . I knew I'd spend the next three days glued to his side. This is how he first met Keaton.

Jim was asked by a producer, who sent out shows to tour summer theaters, if he would like to manage one of these tours on the road. The stars were usually older actors, formerly well-known in films, and still remembered by the public.

Jim Karen said, "I'd love to do that!" The producer asked what star he would like to work with, and Jim said, "Buster Keaton." "Oh, I think he's dead," said the man. "No," Jim replied. "He's very much alive."

Jim contacted Buster, who signed on for it. The play they found was *Merton of the Movies*, set in the 1920s. Perfect! So every day, all summer, Jim spent his time with Keaton. Their friendship grew, and many years after that Jim was often at his ranch in LA.

One day, the two of them were playing cards in Buster's backyard when they heard a car horn at the front of the house. When they went to investigate, they found a white limousine. The door opened.

Bounding out came Jacques Tati . . . another silent clown. Tati had never met Keaton. Nonetheless, he embraced Buster, kissed him on both cheeks, and spoke, excitedly, in French. Keaton did not speak French. Tati did not speak English. After a somewhat confusing moment, Tati went back to his limo and was on his way.

As Jim Karen told me this story, I couldn't help thinking what Tati was likely to be saying to Keaton . . . "When I was just a little boy, I watched you on film and thought 'someday I want to be like him.'" I thought it was a great story.

~

Sometime later, I was invited to attend an evening at the Egyptian Theatre, a landmark in Hollywood, devoted to showing silent films. That evening, one of Keaton's films was shown, then I briefly spoke to the audience about having worked with Keaton in a commercial.

I shared with them the story of Keaton's meeting with Jacques Tati. When I came to the part where Jacques Tati was, most likely, telling Buster about how he watched him as a child, I found myself choked up with tears in my eyes and, for a moment, unable to speak.

What had happened was that the words I imagined Tati speaking to Keaton were the words I had always wanted to say to Buster myself.

~

For a long time, the distance between Sarah and myself had concerned me, not for myself, I had moved on with my life, but for Robin and Adam. I decided to write her a letter, a kind of olive branch. I said I knew that she had sometimes come to California to visit Adam and his family and asked if she would consider sitting down with me to clear the air . . . to make peace, knowing it would mean a lot to Adam and Robin that their parents were putting the past behind them.

I don't know if she got my letter. I only know there was no reply.

~

Back in West Virginia, my brother had fallen ill. Over the next few weeks, I returned home several times since he was in and out of the hospital a lot. He had been diagnosed with bladder cancer; there was also a heart problem, but it wasn't possible for doctors to operate because of the cancer.

It turned out that his cancer had begun to spread. He was now terminal and was sent home. He had around-the-clock nurses, was being given oxygen, and had an IV drip with morphine. I was there at the end with Chuck's wife, Ellen, and their daughter, Gail.

I was talking about Chuck to my son, Adam, who had never met my brother. After hearing about the incident when my brother, at sixteen, had had a fight with my dad and left home, Adam thought that event, and a few other stories, would make a good movie. I wasn't convinced but agreed to give it a try. We called it *The Summer My Brother Left Home*.

We worked on it for maybe six months, and it was a wonderful time. Creating the story together was a real bonding experience. Adam turned out to be a very good writer and contributed many excellent, very cinematic scenes to the story. Many of the memories in this book were a part of it. Adam continued to be extremely funny, and the wordplay and jokes that we shared were a delight.

I admired my brother a lot. Chuck was a natural leader, he was inventive, he was very good mechanically, and he was ambitious. At one point he opened a motorcycle shop, mostly for repairs, but it became so successful that he enlarged the business to a showroom where he sold new motorcycles as well.

Our script has not yet found a home, but writing the screenplay brought us closer, and that, in itself, made it worth it.

43
Keeping Up with Broadway

About three times a year my wife and I go to Manhattan for about ten days. We see a Broadway play every night. That way we can see the best shows and, over the year, catch up on the highlights of the season.

We often have dinner with friends we have in common, such as Lynne Lipton. For lunches Winnie sees her other girlfriends and I get together with Bob Dishy and MacIntyre Dixon.

On our New York trips, Winnie will often spend a day as guest teacher with the kids at the NYU Musical Theatre Program, where she herself had studied. She loves teaching and shares with them her experiences as a professional writer.

~

Winnie had always admired writer Cameron Crowe. His film, *Almost Famous*, based on his experiences traveling with rock bands as a young reporter in the 1960s, set the stage for his career. Cameron reached out to Winnie to join him on his new TV-series, *Roadies*, as co-producer and writer. Cameron loved *My So-Called Life* and had long been a fan of Winnie's writing. His most successful film, of course, is *Jerry Maguire*. Winnie, in fact, played a small part in the film. Working with Cameron was a labor of love.

~

Probably the most requested photograph I sign my name to is not even a picture of me . . . it's a photograph of Sarge the World War II Jeep, in the movie *Cars* (2006). Many of these photos are for someone's kid. Young boys, especially, seem to love Sarge.

I recorded the dialogue for *Cars* (2006) in about two hours, and the animators then began their incredible work bringing Sarge to life. It was a long time after that before I saw the finished film and finally heard my voice coming out of the Jeep. The process was similar for the sequels I recorded; *Cars 2* (2011), and later *Cars 3* (2017), but the long wait was worth it seeing the character come to life in each film.

My voice can also be heard in a lot of toy Sarge Jeeps . . . and if you visit the Radiator Springs Racers Attraction (located in Cars Land at Disney California Adventure Park at the Disneyland Resort) kids can ride in bigger versions of many Radiator Springs cars. In the Jeep, my voice as Sarge will talk to anyone taking a ride, saying, "Ten Hut! We have a visitor!"

For me, it's been a fun ride too.

~

My sister, Patty, had married young. She had two sons, Steve and Joe, and a daughter, Cathy. Sadly, her husband, Bill, passed away in his forties. Once her kids were grown and out of the house, she lived alone. She never met another man, and I thought she was quite lonely, although she never complained.

On a visit home I was at her house. Looking around, even I was depressed. Her living room was paneled with a dark walnut plywood, and the lighting was also very dim. I realized the easy chair she sat in, and the TV she watched, would have to remind her of her husband and her children. I made a decision, on the spot, to buy her a new place to live . . . a place without so many memories.

My niece Gail, who was in real estate, was a smart young woman. I liked her a lot. She helped me find a house for my sister; it was brand new and close to Gail's house . . . it seemed to be perfect! I suggested to Patty that she get rid of her furniture and appliances and other reminders of the old house and start anew. Except for family photos and other personal items, her next home would be completely new, including the furniture.

After that, each time I called her she'd tell me, "Every day when I wake up and walk into my new kitchen, I am so happy." Which made me happy too. Now I was able to share with Patty her new home. She told me she loved every room in her home, and her yard, and her flowers. She never once before this had ever seemed happy, and now she was. She lived there for five years before she passed away, but for her, those were five very good years. I was glad I had been able to make that possible for her.

~

In an interview, a journalist once asked me how many commercials I had done. I said, "Oh, I've probably done one for every product from A to Z." I didn't mean it literally. He said, "I'd like to see that list." We were meeting a week later to get some photographs for the magazine. I looked through my datebooks and found I could, indeed, make such a list. Even for the difficult letters, like Q, X, Y, and Z (Quazar, Xerox, Yellow Pages, and Zenith).

Many years later, long after I'd done my last commercial, I found a box in my attic with all my datebooks (I save a lot of stuff). I had some time on my hands, so I decided, just for laughs, and since so many people ask me about it, to make a complete list.

My commercial career lasted for about fifteen years. I had always had Week-at-a-Glance datebooks. In those books I had written down all my auditions, with a check mark added when I booked the job. The total came to more than 620.* About 75 percent of them were for radio. The rest were voice-overs and on-camera. It seems unbelievable, but it's true.

---

* For anyone who's interested, the entire list can be found on my website: www.paul dooleyactor.com.

I'm a fairly patient person, and I try not to let things annoy me, but I do have a pet peeve. There's a kind of commercial I just can't stand; they're for prescription drugs, and they're always the same. The drug being pushed has a lot of *side effects* . . . none of them good. Watching one of these ads you will see and hear:

A beautiful backyard, an inviting home, and an attractive couple emerges smiling broadly as a voice tells you about the benefits of the drug and its side effects. To offset the warning of what could go wrong, a laughing young girl runs onto the screen, embraces her overjoyed father, as we hear:

"May cause hives, blisters, nausea, vomiting . . ."

Then, as an excited young boy comes running in to join this festival of fun and hug his ecstatic mom, we hear:

". . . drowsiness, diarrhea, constipation . . ."

The family begins to dance around in elation.

". . . difficulty breathing, difficulty not breathing, heart failure . . ."

Just then, joining the family, a prizewinning golden retriever comes bounding in.

". . . with a possible chance of death."

Now . . . who *wouldn't* want to take that pill?

~

Oh, I forgot, one other pet peeve. In the shower, in the soap dish, I'll sometimes find what's left of a bar of soap. What was once a real bar of soap, with *hopes and dreams*, is now reduced to a sliver. That's right. A *sliver*. The ghost of a soap now haunting the soap dish. I desperately want to get rid of it but feel guilty about it . . . after all, it's still soap, and it will still make lather.

What to do?

I think you can see my problem.

~

What do actors think of other actors? First, they are our teachers, and we study them. Having had very little formal training in acting, I learned from watching other actors . . . and by applying those lessons to my own work. I would guess this is true of a lot of actors.

As my own acting evolved, I found I was drawn to actors whose style was simpler, more natural. There are many actors whose style is quite robust, kind of over-the-top, and that's fine . . . for them. Personally, I have chosen to follow the dictum "less-is-more."

One of the actors who embodies this is the great Anthony Hopkins. His acting is so natural; it's the kind of acting I like to do. In fact, a critic once compared me to Anthony Hopkins. He said . . . "He's no Anthony Hopkins."

I'm sometimes described as an actor who doesn't show his emotions . . . (Thanks, Dad!) I've been called repressed and taciturn. I'm not *exactly* like that . . . but it's close enough.

My friends like to kid me about it.

"Were you the model for Mount Rushmore?"
"No . . . I think you mean Stonehenge."

~

Aside from the great silent movie comics, I enjoyed a collection of character actors from the movies in the 1940s, all of them adept at comedy. They were Franklin Pangborn, Edgar Kennedy, Frank McHugh, Grady Sutton, and Sig Ruman. A particular place in my heart belongs to a select group of sketch actors. They are Martin Short, Tim Conway, and Harvey Korman. Another great, old-school sketch comic was Bert Lahr, who spent years in vaudeville and in Broadway revues. Still, he is best remembered as the Cowardly Lion in *The Wizard of Oz*.

Allow me to apologize in advance for naming a lot of men and almost no women. This is simply because I am a man. Let me just check . . . yeah, I'm a man, and my role models were other male character actors, especially those who leaned toward comedy.

Later, the film world discovered the talented Charles Durning; I consider him the King of Character Actors. In 2007, he was given a Lifetime Achievement Award by the Screen Actors Guild—the only character actor to be so honored. I had the privilege of working with him onstage at the Garry Marshall Theatre.

Let me now praise funny women, all of them exquisitely gifted: Catherine O'Hara, Andrea Martin, Lily Tomlin, Sarah Silverman, Melissa McCarthy, Julia Louis-Dreyfus, and the late Madeline Kahn and Cloris Leachman.

I would also like to salute the most brilliant, most influential dramatic actors in film history. Marlon Brando changed film acting forever when he first appeared in *A Streetcar Named Desire* (and later in *The Godfather*).

Robert DeNiro astonished the film world in *Taxi Driver* and *Raging Bull*, both directed by Martin Scorsese, and myriad other roles over the years.

Al Pacino revealed an incredible range in his acting from the young college student Michael Corleone to the head of the Mafia, also in *The*

Godfather. That being said, I personally believe his performance in *Dog Day Afternoon* is equally brilliant . . . perhaps even his best.

Watching Philip Seymour Hoffman, recently, for the fourth time, in his epic portrayal of Truman Capote, in the movie *Capote*, he went *so deep* into his character that he completely transformed himself in the part.

The great Anthony Hopkins has a history of magnificent performances on film from *Remains of the Day* to *Silence of the Lambs*, where he played a menacing psychopath (and still underplayed it to perfection), and finally, in his most recent role in *The Father*, he played an older man with dementia, which brought me to tears, and in my opinion, he was never better . . . as witness, his Oscar for Best Actor.

Those five actors, I consider, to be the "Royal Family of Film."

~

Aside from parties, Winnie and I never wrote or performed anything together professionally until we wrote a play for ourselves. We worked on it for several months. We would be the only actors but would each play two parts. It was a comedy/drama. We opened the play, *One of Your Biggest Fans,* * in 2013 at the Odyssey Theatre in LA.

We had only one other professional collaboration. A fundraising event asked ten TV writers to each contribute a ten-minute play. Winnie was busy but said she'd do it if I helped her. I said, "Okay."

I'm not sure which of us thought of the idea, but it would become a short parody of *Love Letters* by A. R. Gurney, which had been done hundreds of times. There were only two actors, a man and a woman, who read aloud letters they had written to each other over a lifetime. There was no scenery, just two chairs. The actors never needed to memorize anything.

---

* Both *One of Your Biggest Fans* and *Post-Its* are published by Playscripts, Inc.

Our parody was called *Post-Its: Notes on a Marriage.** Our couple would read aloud fifty years' worth of Post-its. Winnie and I first performed it at the Tiffany Theater in LA, and since then, it has been performed well over a hundred times all over the country.

44
Comedians . . . Old and New

With my continuing interest in all things comic, I made it my business to track comedians and their jokes and to follow the comedy trajectory over the past seventy-five years. For a long time, jokes were written by writers and paid for by comics. Bob Hope is a perfect example; he always had writers. The jokes were much the same; mother-in-law jokes, my wife's cooking jokes, bad airline food, and so on. I never found him funny.

In the mid-1960s, there was a big change. The new young comedians didn't really rely on writers; they found their jokes by talking honestly about their own lives. This came to be called "observational" comedy. I discovered and embraced this new breed of stand-up comics. They were sharper, brighter, and more intelligent, with material that "said something." The genesis can be traced to a couple of influential comedians . . . one was Robert Klein, another was Richard Pryor; they became the forerunners of the new style. They both began to do concerts, Robert Klein had the very first HBO comedy special, and Richard Pryor also did concerts and TV specials.

Pryor actually changed comedy in a profound way. His material was so personal, so honest, and it revealed so much pain that the audience not only laughed at him but also loved him.

To back up a bit, there was lovable Bob Newhart. Very shy. Very dry. Strange but super smart, Woody Allen, and weird and wonderful Jonathan Winters. George Carlin was an excellent wordsmith, and just as Lenny Bruce had, he used "dirty words." His list of the "seven words you can't say on TV" turned the comedy world upside down. There was high-energy Billy Crystal with his uncanny impressions, and Rodney Dangerfield, better at "jokes for joke's sake" than almost anyone.

Let us not forget Mel Brooks and Carl Reiner with their *2000 Year Old Man*. I also loved *Beyond the Fringe*, and the *Monty Pythons*.

Beloved Johnny Carson, the architect of late-night; David Letterman, the godfather to many young comedians, and mischievous, provocative, and very funny; Jay Leno, who got his laughs by laughing himself; and finally Stephen Colbert, bright, political satirist, and whip smart, a worthy heir to Johnny Carson's throne.

Garry Shandling, the anxious, perfectionist, reclusive, and spiritual funny fellow, and extremely smart Steve Martin, sometimes surreal and often just plain silly. Jerry Seinfeld also had an observational style but with a rhythm all his own. Steven Wright, who is not so much a performer as just a guy telling us what he wrote . . . and he wrote great! So original, so smart.

I love Chris Rock, his energetic style, his evangelical cadence, the way he stalks the stage . . . how he owns his audience.

And, of course, the remarkable Robin Williams, with his mile-a-minute mind and his scattershot style, his versatility, and his voices. Amazing!

Have I left anybody out?

Probably.

～

Just for myself (and obviously now for you), I compiled a history of the greatest silent comedy masters of all time. The "classic" silent comedy era started in 1914 with Chaplin, Keaton, and Harry Langdon and ended in 1929 when sound was added and "movies" were now "talkies" (Chaplin still made a number of successful silent comedies through 1936). It would be another twenty-four years before the next silent clown appeared on film.

Fast-forward to 1953, when a new master of pantomime came along. He was the tall, thin, very funny French comedian Jacques Tati, in a film called *Mr. Hulot's Holiday*. He went on to make a handful of other films. Although there were a few words heard here and there, these were largely silent movies. He was highly entertaining, and his bits of physical comedy could easily have played well in the 1920s.

In 1955, the famous French performer Marcel Marceau came to New York with his show. He was the first classical mime I'd ever seen. He came from the tradition of that ancient art in Paris. He returned to America several times, and I went to see all his shows . . . and he was, as usual, brilliant!

Dick Van Dyke was hardly a silent comic. In his popular 1961 TV show, he did a lot of talking, but previously, on the Broadway stage, and later in a number of films, he certainly showed his skills as a physical comedian.

Van Dyke began performing in an act called The Merry Mimes with his brother, Jerry. They had a "record" act in which they pantomimed and "lip-synched" to records. He, too, could have easily worked in silent films.

In fact, Dick Van Dyke later played a silent movie comic in a film called *The Comic*, directed by Carl Reiner. His character in that film is loosely based on Keaton. It had been six years since Marcel Marceau.

A young man named Bill Irwin, a clown who worked silently, opened on Broadway in his own show. He had, for a few years, been a part of the Pickle Family Circus, a one-ring circus in San Francisco with lots of clowns. He worked in the tradition of the great silent comics and was obviously influenced by Keaton, and later, he did a number of other highly regarded clown shows on Broadway. The critics loved Bill and his shows. He received the MacArthur Genius Award for his work. It had been more than twenty years since Dick Van Dyke.

In this history of silent comedy I was studying, there came one more actor who qualified. It was now six years since Bill Irwin.

The new guy was Michael Richards. Yes, the fellow who played Kramer on *Seinfeld*. Of course, he also talked, but his physical comedy was amazing. Kramer made an entrance through Jerry's door many, many times, yet, every time he did it, his moves were slightly different and always hilarious. He, too, of course, could have held his own in silent films.

So, you see how, throughout a *hundred-year span*, great visual comedy masters were few and far between.

~

A comedian is usually said to have good *timing*. And a great comedian will have *great timing . . .* but what is timing?

It's the way in which a performer uses cadence and rhythm in the delivery of his jokes to emphasize the humor. It's most often instinctive. A comic is probably born with his own timing. However, experience and practice can also sharpen that skill.

Jack Benny is considered by many to be the master of slow timing . . . in other words, using long pauses to point up his jokes. On the other hand, a very quick rhythm can also be a kind of timing. I personally think the best use of timing in a comedy routine is in the classic "Who's on First?" by Abbott and Costello. That sketch is not exactly smart, it is in fact almost stupid . . . but the pacing, the tempo, and especially the *timing* is just perfect! In fact, I think of it as . . . comedy music.

~

These are a few of my favorite words:

> Picayune: An Icelandic custom wherein a young healthy yune is chosen and sacrificed to the gods.

> Scallywag: A gentleman who enjoys, from time to time, wagging his scally . . . often in public.

Ragamuffin: The specialty of a Scottish bakery. A scone-like breakfast treat, traditionally served in a washcloth.

Cockamamie (also Cock 'o Mamie): A British pub, so named for its proprietor Mamie, advertising her pride in her husband's penis.

~

A few more of my favorite words, now strung together to form a sentence or two, creating a joke, or two:

Why are elephants wrinkled? Nobody wants to iron them. —Anonymous

I used up all my sick days, now I just call in dead. —Anonymous

As Dr. Jekyll said to Mr. Hyde, "You wait here, I'll go change!" —Anonymous

George Burns at ninety said . . . . "At my age, my back goes out more often than I do."

Never go to a doctor whose office plants have died. —Erma Bombeck

In real life there is no such thing as Algebra. —Fran Liebowitz

I've been on so many blind dates, I should get a free dog. —Wendy Liebman

My wife's an earth sign. I'm a water sign. Together we make mud. —Rodney Dangerfield

There are three things not listed on my résumé. They are not accomplishments, just exciting things that happened to happen to me.

I made a commercial with Buster Keaton.

I shook hands with Charlie Chaplin.

I made a comedy album with Cassius Clay . . . later known as Muhammad Ali.

Oh, and I once did a commercial with Margaret Hamilton . . . the original "Wicked Witch of the West."

Another big moment was backstage in 2016 after a performance of *Hamilton*, the once-in-a-generation Broadway sensation! My wife had already met the star and creator of the show, Lin-Manuel Miranda . . . at the time, the biggest "star" in the biggest "hit" on Broadway.

She wanted to say hello. As the two of them chatted, I stood off to one side near them. He glanced over at me, seemed surprised, and said, "You're Paul Dooley!" Winnie said, "Yes, he's my husband." Lin-Manuel laughed. We all talked for a few minutes, then he had to go say hello to his other admirers. In parting, he said to me, "Paul Dooley . . . you've made my day!"

Later, Winnie smiled and said, "You know, today's the day his show received sixteen Tony nominations, but *you* . . . made his day."

When asked if I would ever write a book, I always said no. Instead, I created a one-man stage show, *Movie Dad*. We opened the show in Hollywood and had a successful run.

I'm a collector of well-known jokes, some of which you would only hear in a bar, a locker room, or at an office around the watercooler. No one knows how they started, they're just handed down by word of mouth. Most of them are off-color, but for my show, I picked a couple that seemed okay.

You all remember Quasimodo . . . the man who lived in the bell tower of Notre Dame. His only job was to ring the big bell every hour. One day he was distracted. He pulled the big rope, the bell swung back. When Quasimodo forgot to step aside, the bell came forward and *knocked him out of the tower* and down to the street. A crowd gathered. A policeman came over:

"Does anyone know this man?"

"Well, I don't know his name . . . but his face rings a bell."

While Quasimodo was recovering, his brother Queasy-modo took his place in the tower. On the first day, *the same thing happened again.* The bell knocked *him* out of the tower and onto the street. A crowd gathered. A policeman came over (probably the same guy):

"Does anyone know this man?"

"Well, I don't know his name . . . but he's a dead ringer for his brother!"

I had told these jokes often, but only to two or three people at a time. Sometimes I'd get a nice laugh, often just a chuckle . . . but when that audience of about a hundred people heard it, that laugh came roaring back to me like a tidal wave. That response was thrilling.

I was drawn, strangely, to these two tales of Quasimodo. Savannah pointed out to me that I am, myself . . . a kind of Quasimodo.

For years, people have said those very same words to me, countless times: "I don't know your name, but your face rings a bell." I didn't mind being told that. I thought it was fine; it was enough that they knew my face.

45
Getting Back to Buster

The theater in Hollywood where I first performed my one-man show was called *Sacred Fools*. To my amazement, it turned out to be just *one block away* from *Buster Keaton's original studio*, and the building that housed the theater had once been a space for Buster's office. Quite a coincidence.

I'd also learned that, in Keaton's divorce, his ex-wife took the house, took the kids, and even changed their names . . . they were *no longer Keatons*. Just as *my* ex-wife, when she took off with *my* kids had also changed *their* names . . . they were *no longer Dooleys*.

Sometimes I wonder if—I know it sounds crazy—but maybe, in some past life, I was in silent films. And maybe . . . I knew Keaton.

It would explain a lot.

I mean, why do I love him so much? Why am I so drawn to him? Finally, it came to me.

My dad was a man of few words.

Buster was a man of no words.

I never saw my father smile.

Same as Buster.

Then I realized . . . Buster Keaton had long ago become *my role model*, my surrogate father who *never smiled*, but who *made me smile*, and who made me love him.

Later, I did the show again at Theatre West in LA for another four weeks. I had rewritten the script, trying to make it better. At my final performance of the show something strange happened. My wife noticed I seemed to be speaking and moving a lot slower than usual and was even a little off-balance. I did, however, finish the show.

Afterwards, we went straight to the ER. My heart rate was below thirty, and without asking my permission I was given a pacemaker. I've had it for four years, and now I hardly know it's there.

I have been lucky to live a long life, and I am generally in good health. But at some point, the body begins, like an old car, to *fall apart*. For me, it was when I turned seventy.

I had always been at risk for diabetes. On my mother's side, there was a carnival of diabetes. Her parents had it, she and her eight siblings had it, and my brother and sister had it. As a family, we were known for it. Foolishly, I paid no attention to diabetes for . . . oh, about seventy years. I was finally diagnosed with the disease (it was called adult-onset diabetes, or Type 2, and it is now kept under control with medication).

Next came hearing loss. After about a year of saying, "How's that again?" I succumbed to wearing a hearing aid. Great! Now I could pick up the sound of *my own footsteps*, kids *playing loudly* next door, *everyone* in a crowded restaurant. For me it was a disaster! I returned to, "How's that again?"

On the set of a film, if I were waiting outside a door for my entrance, they would set up a tiny warning light that blinked when I had to enter. Another solution for me was, if I were in a scene with other actors, I'd wait for their lips to stop moving . . . then I'd say my line.

When my eyesight started going, I had laser surgery to fix it, after which I had 20/20 vision. I thought of my father. If that procedure had been available to him, he might have seen the world . . . in a whole new light.

In general, I'm doing fine. I'm not sure of my *sell-by date*, but I'm doing fine.

Now in my nineties and grateful to be in good health, I began to think of those who are no longer here . . . the ones I'd lost.

My father, my mother, my sister, my brother; my teenage gang, Harold, Junie, and Ab; partners Jim Dukas, Bob Lichello, and David Panich; my therapist Dan Kaplowitz; my companion Margery Bond;

fellow actors Beatrice Arthur, Doris Roberts, Charlotte Rae, Jimmy Boyd, Dom DeLuise, Orson Bean, Tom Poston, and James Karen; fellow writers Emily Levine and Pat McCormick; fellow improvisers Richard Libertini, Sevren Darden, and Lewis Arquette; and Robin Williams, astonishing comedian, talented actor, and a gentle soul. Another great loss was filmmaker Robert Altman and his wife, Kathryn.

46
COVID-19!
Coronavirus!
Quarantined!

On March 10, our world changed. We were suddenly housebound, but something else happened too. Broadway went dark. *Wicked* was no more. Our primary source of income had disappeared. We started to cut back on our spending, but the future was unknown; our home had become our refuge.

Winnie and I used the quarantine as an opportunity to change our diet to eat in a healthier way: more fruits and vegetables, a little fish and chicken but very little red meat. Over the next year I would lose twenty-five pounds, and now I feel better than I have in years.

Once the isolation began, nearly everything in show business shut down. There would be no new movies or TV shows produced. However, Winnie had a script she needed to complete.

Because of *HUGE*, Winnie and Savannah were often hired as a writing team, so Winnie's new story became one they could work on together, while apart, with a lot of phone calls, emails, and Zoom meetings. On her own, Savannah had another project she was working on, and, as always, Winnie would be working on the screenplay for *Wicked*.

I knew I wouldn't be doing any acting for quite a while, so I decided to expand my one-man show into a book, the book you're reading now, or the book you found you *could put down* and is now just a doorstop.

I'm not sure why I'm writing a book about my life, anyway . . .

I can't even spell Mem-war.

My one-man show was mostly comic; after all, there was a live audience, and I wanted to go for the laughs. A book, of course, is a very different thing. I would still include humor, but as I began writing, especially about my parents, my childhood and the Depression, my story became more serious with anecdotes from those early years, and I wondered if I was up to the task.

Still, I kept writing, never knowing if I'd find a publisher. After six months I had about a hundred pages. Then, a friend of ours, Robert Freedman, mentioned my name to John Cerullo, the senior executive editor at Applause Books. They specialize in books about theater and film, and show business in general. They agreed to publish my book.

So, as I write this, I am ninety-three years old. I don't use a computer. I'm writing it by hand . . . in cursive. Although, I briefly considered a quill.

~

A sense of humor can go a long way, especially during a lockdown. I'm sure many couples are likely to have disagreements when isolated like this, which I can understand. My wife and I just happen to be compatible. This is not meant to imply we're the perfect couple. Of course, we can annoy each other; we're only human. A passing remark can be taken as a slight and may seem insensitive. The key thing is, if you've hurt the feelings of a loved one, even without meaning to, just *own up* to it . . . and apologize.

In retrospect, if I had been wiser, more empathetic, even more evolved in my earlier relationships, perhaps I would have been a better partner. But as I've grown, I've learned.

~

As I'm writing this, I'm trying to recall some memories, long forgotten, about the time I lived happily in Brooklyn with my kids but found . . .

I could *not* remember much about it. I thought, *What kind of a father am I not to remember?*

My wife, who is very intuitive and has a keen understanding of people, told me it was likely that after my kids were gone, and I went through the pain of that, I needed to minimize those memories.

I think she was right.

For quite a while I had come to see myself as this repressed, stoic sort of character that I had sometimes played in films. When my wife saw that I was defining myself that way, she shared with me what she thought was closer to the truth.

As a teenager, she had seen me in commercials on TV when I was much younger. She told me that, back then, I was more lighthearted, breezy, and upbeat . . . that I'd even smiled.

She believes that once I lost my kids, I became more serious, more somber, and not just because I was turning into my father, as I had thought, but even more, because the pain of losing my kids had left its mark on me.

~

The lockdown brought my wife and me closer, made us more grateful to have each other. This has been true with Robin, still living back East, and Adam and Savannah, who both live near us. Our concerns for one another have also strengthened our emotional ties. We found a new appreciation of our family and a generosity of spirit which we share that has meant a lot to all of us.

I'm grateful that Adam lives so close by, and even in lockdown we're able to spend time together safely. I also keep in touch with Savannah, masked and at a distance. And I speak often by phone with Robin.

~

Hooray! It's 2021! Winnie and I have both been vaccinated, as have Adam and Savannah, and we are now able to safely enjoy hugs. The freedom of being able to do that felt so good. Robin and Elias have also been vaccinated, and we are looking forward to a visit from them soon. As our life begins to open up and has, at least, a semblance of "getting back to normal," we are all hopeful.

47
Reflections

Despite that one devastating time without my kids, I feel I've had a pretty good life. My career has been rewarding, and I *did* get my kids back and was able to start over. I married a wonderful woman, and we have a daughter who is just as sweet as her mother.

Savannah was a gift. She was the one who was not taken from me, the one who was just *there*, which allowed me to spend her entire childhood with her . . . I had been given a second chance.

Looking back on my life, both professionally and personally, I know now that *this* . . . is who I *really* am.

fa·ther

/ˈfäTHər/

Noun

A man who provides for his family and cares for his children.

But . . . enough about me.

Acknowledgments

When Savannah was quite young, my wife and I were able to drive her to and from school. When Winnie went into production for *My So-Called Life* and I got busy doing movies, we found a young woman, Shauna Marlin, who would pick up our daughter from school at three o'clock, bring her home, give her a bite to eat, and be there until we got home.

Shauna was so capable and so reliable, we later expanded her duties to include household tasks, bookkeeping, monitoring our medications, and later handling ticket requests for *Wicked*, as well as countless other responsibilities. She became invaluable to us. In addition, Shauna is a kindhearted person, a kind of an Earth Mother. She's been with us for more than twenty-five years now, and she has become a member of our family. We don't know what we'd do without her.

A friend of Winnie's recommended a housekeeper. Veda turned out to be a treasure. She takes care of our home as if it were her own and even tends to our flowers. We love her and are grateful that she has been in our lives for more than ten years.

I like to take care of things around the house, but there are projects I can't always do myself. I got to know this handyman, Frank Velazquez, but he's not just a handyman, he's a jack-of-all-trades and master of, well, everything. Over the last fifteen years he has been my eyes and my hands. If I can imagine or design anything, he can execute it. He's done more than a hundred jobs, large and small, for me, inside and outside the house.

Three blocks from our home there was a Pilates studio. Winnie went to check it out and decided to start taking classes. She suggested I join her. I was never an exercise guy, never went to the gym, but I went just once to see what it was like.

I wasn't interested in the classes (it seemed like a lot of work), but I was impressed by the instructor. I found him, Bruce Burchmore, to be a kindred spirit. He was very funny. Like me, he loved wordplay and comedy. I was hooked. I started classes.

Bruce would take me through one exercise perfectly imitating Sean Connery, another sounding like Homer Simpson, or Mr. Magoo, or one of the Beatles. Every session was like a ping-pong game of jokes and celebrity voices. I never learned to love all that stretching, but I stretched it out for more than ten years.

Beginning in 1980, Jeffrey Rosenhouse, my CPA, also became my business manager and, wisely, found opportunities to make investments on my behalf. He also set up a pension plan for the future, and, for forty years he has advised me and Winnie on all of our finances and has done so extremely well. Our entire family appreciates Jeff's guidance.

We found a primary care doctor, Ronald Sue, and have been taken care of by him for twenty-five years. People sometimes describe a doctor as having a "bedside manner." Well, Ron has never made a "house call" or been anywhere near my bedside . . . but he has been the most concerned, most caring, almost fatherly doctor we could have ever hoped for.

One day, a miracle came to our front door. Her name was Fiona Lakeland. It was 2015.

She had been recommended to us by our friend Bruce, who knew we were looking for a new assistant. Fiona is an actress and a writer. She is attractive, charming, and, well, sort of a genius. She would schedule meetings, then reschedule them when necessary, order things online, return them when necessary. Take messages, arrange appointments, cancel them when necessary. Print stuff, recycle paper . . . well, you get the idea. All this was done with unfailing cheerfulness and remarkable efficiency. Fiona is whip-smart and never needs a to-do list; she keeps it all in her head.

Eventually, she produced my one-man show, and as I began my book, she became my alter ego, my voice. Since I don't use a computer, our process is as follows: I write every day, then dictate my pages to Fiona by phone, and once a week she prints out a new version of my work and sends it to me. She also acts as an editor. She knows the manuscript like the back of her lovely hand.

She has been invaluable to me. Without her, this book may have been . . . just a pamphlet.

And finally, but certainly not least, I would like to acknowledge my publishing team at Applause Books. John Cerullo (former senior executive editor) and Carol Flannery (former senior acquisitions editor) were instrumental in getting things started; I'm very grateful for their confidence in what the book would become. Additionally, Chris Chappel (senior acquisitions editor), Barbara Claire (editorial assistant), Laurel Meyers (editorial assistant), Megan Murray (production editor), and the entire team at Applause Books have all been wonderful to work with.

Filmography
(Abridged)

The Out of Towners (1970)—Hotel Clerk, *with Jack Lemmon*

Death Wish (1974)—Cop at Hospital

Slap Shot (1977)—Hockey Announcer, *with Paul Newman*

A Wedding (1978)—*with Carol Burnett and Mia Farrow; directed by Robert Altman*

A Perfect Couple (1979)—*with Marta Heflin; directed by Robert Altman*

Breaking Away (1979)—Dad, *with Dennis Christopher; directed by Peter Yates; screenplay by Steve Tesich*

Health (1980)—Dr. Gil Gainey, *with Carol Burnett, James Garner, Glenda Jackson, and Lauren Bacall; directed by Robert Altman*

Popeye (1980)—Wimpy, *with Robin Williams and Shelley Duvall; directed by Robert Altman; screenplay by Jules Feiffer*

Kiss Me Goodbye (1982)—*with Jeff Bridges*

Strange Brew (1983)—Claude Elsinore, *with Max von Sydow*

Sixteen Candles (1984)—Jim Baker, *with Molly Ringwald; directed by John Hughes*

Filmography (Abridged)

OC and Stiggs (1985)—Randall Schwab, *with Cynthia Nixon and Jon Cryer; directed by Robert Altman*

Shakes the Clown (1991)—*with Bobcat Goldthwait*

My Boyfriend's Back (1993)—Big Chuck, *with Philip Seymour Hoffman and Cloris Leachman; directed by Bob Balaban*

Waiting for Guffman (1996)—UFO Abductee, *with Catherine O'Hara, Eugene Levy, Parker Posey, and Christopher Guest; directed by Christopher Guest*

Angels in the Endzone (1997)—Coach Buck

Clockwatchers (1997)—Bud Chapman, *with Toni Collette*

Happy Texas (1999)—The Judge, *with William H. Macy*

Runaway Bride (1999)—*with Julia Roberts, Richard Gere, and Joan Cusack*

Insomnia (2002)—*with Al Pacino, Robin Williams, and Hilary Swank*

A Mighty Wind (2003)—*directed by Christopher Guest*

Come Away Home (2005)—Grandpa Donald Brooks, *with Lea Thompson and Thomas Gibson*

Cars (2006), *Cars 2* (2011), *Cars 3* (2017)—*voice of* "Sarge"

For Your Consideration (2006)—*directed by Christopher Guest*

Hairspray (2007)—*with John Travolta, Michelle Pfeiffer, and Christopher Walken*

Horsemen (2009)—Father Whiteleather, *with Dennis Quaid*

Other People (2016)—*with Molly Shannon and Jesse Plemons*

The Great Buster (2018)—Self (documentary), *with Mel Brooks, Dick Van Dyke, Frank Capra, and Peter Bogdanovich; directed by Bogdanovich*

Saving Paradise (2021)—Gramps

TV Shows
(Abridged)

The Tonight Show (1959)

The Ed Sullivan Show (1963)—*with Sid Caesar, and with Richard Libertini*

The Jack Paar Program (1964)—*with Bob Dishy*

The Defenders (1964)—"Conflict of Interests"

The Merv Griffin Show (1966–1980)—many episodes

Bewitched (1966)—"Oedipus Hex"

The Dom DeLuise Show (1968)—Season One

Jules Feiffer's Hold Me (1981)—TV movie

Faerie Tale Theatre (1982–1983)

Spenser: For Hire (1985)—"Resurrection"

The Golden Girls (1986–1987)—"Love, Rose"; "Empty Nest"

The Murder of Mary Phagan (1988)—TV miniseries

Lip Service (1988)—TV movie

Alf (1987–1989)—many episodes

Coming of Age (1988–1989)—many episodes

thirtysomething (1990)—"The Go Between"; "Samurai Ad Man"

Coach (1991)—"A Father and Son Reunion"

TV Shows (Abridged)

The Wonder Years (1991)—"Soccer"

Pros and Cons (1991)—"Ho! Ho! Hold up!"

Mother of the Bride (1993)—TV movie

Tales of the City (1993)—TV miniseries

The Boys (1993)—"Ninety-Five in the Shade"

Tales from the Crypt (1993)—"Forever Ambergris"

L.A. Law (1993)—"Safe Sex"

The Mommies (1994)—"The Old Man Cometh"

State of Emergency (1994)—TV movie *with Joe Mantegna*

Dream On (1992–1994)—many episodes

Chicago Hope (1994)—"Over the Rainbow"

My So-Called Life (1994)—"Father Figures"; "Self-Esteem"

Ellen (1996)—"Lobster Diary," *with Ellen DeGeneres and Mary Tyler Moore*

Grace Under Fire (1994–1996)—many episodes, *with Brett Butler*

Millenium (1996)—"The Well-Worn Lock"

Star Trek: Deep Space Nine (1994–1997)—many episodes

Sleepwalkers (1998)—"Passed Imperfect"

Ally McBeal (2001)—"Reasons to Believe"

Once and Again (2001–2002)—many episodes

The Practice (1999–2002)—many episodes

Law & Order: Criminal Intent (2003)—"Cherry Red"

Becker (2003)—"What's Love Got to Do with It?"

ER (1995–2004)—many episodes

CSI: Crime Scene Investigation (2004)—"Getting Off"

Curb Your Enthusiasm (2000–2005)—many episodes, *with Larry David*

Desperate Housewives (2005)—three episodes, *with Teri Hatcher*

Boston Legal (2007)—*with William Shatner*

Grey's Anatomy (2008)—"Losing My Mind"

Scrubs (2009)—"Our Histories"

Huge (2010)—many episodes

TV Shows (Abridged)

Private Practice (2011)—"Heaven Can Wait"

Hot in Cleveland (2012)—*with Betty White*

Parenthood (2014)—"Promises," *with Craig T. Nelson*

Heartbeat (2016)—"What Happens in Vegas . . . Happens"

The Good Doctor (2017)—"22 Steps"

The Guest Book (2018)—"Killer Party"

The Kids Are Alright (2018–2019)—many episodes

Life in Pieces (2019)—two episodes, *with Dianne Wiest*

Merry Happy Whatever (2019)—"Merry Ex-Mas," *with Dennis Quaid*

Modern Family (2020)—"Dead on a Rival"

Bibliography

Blesh, Rudi. *Keaton*. The McMillan Company, 1966.

Chaplin, Charles. *My Autobiography*. The Penguin Group, New York, 1964.

Curtis, James. *Buster Keaton: A Filmmaker's Life*. Knopf Doubleday Publishing Group, 2022.

Keaton, Buster (with Charles Samuels). *My Wonderful World of Slapstick*. Doubleday & Co., 1960.

Keaton, Eleanor (with Jeffrey Vance). *Buster Keaton Remembered*. Abrams, 2001.

Kerr, Walter. *The Silent Clowns*. Alfred A. Knopf, 1975.

Knight, Arthur. *The Liveliest Art*. McMillan & Company, 1957.

Meade, Marion. *Buster Keaton, Cut to the Chase: A Biography*. Harper Collins, 1995.

Sennett, Mack (as told to Cameron Shipp). *King of Comedy*. Doubleday & Co., 1954.

Starr, Michael Seth. *Art Carney: A Biography*. First Fromm International, 1997.

Stevens, Dana. *Camera Man*. Simon & Schuster, 2022.

Index

Note: Page references to figures are italicized; Photos in photospread are indicated by "p-"

in, 7–8; identity in, 9–10; jokes in, 15–16; Lillian in, 23; memorization in, 17; money in, 14; movies in, 20–21; name in, 5–6, 14; nicknames in, 14; oak tree in, 22–23, *24*; obsession in, 16–17; play space in, 6–7; "Pond Run" in, 22–25, *24*; radio in, 15–17; rain in, 11; sense of humor in, 18; "spying" in, 14–15; Stonewall Inn in, 22; swimming naked in, 23, 25; swing in, 23–25, *24*. *See also* school

childhood home: basement of, 3; coal stove in, 4; foundation of, 3; free rent related to, 4; front porch on, 10; front room of, 4; ice box in, 4; middle room of, 4; outhouse of, 3, 176; rocking chair in, 5; swing at, 10–11; workshop at, 10

children: blame related to, 160; car trouble and, 145–46; custody of, 160, 165; depression over, 162; disappearance of, 159–62; emptiness related to, 160; grief over, 161–62; hopelessness related to, 160–61; imagination about, 161; irony related to, 184–85; kidnapping play with, 158; police related to, 145; postcards from, 158; reminders about, 165; ritual to, 161; shame related to, 161; shock related to, 160–61; "stage," 184; visitations

with, 144–45, 158–59; without closure, 165, 169. *See also* Dooley, Adam; Dooley, Robin

Children's Television Workshop, 146–47. *See also The Electric Company*

children's theatre, 71–72

chores, in childhood, 11

A Christmas Story, 196

Christopher, Dennis, *p-1,* 170, 171, *171,* 173

Chuck. *See* Brown, Charles

Cimino, Michael, 106–7

Clay, Cassius, 244

cliffhanger, 151

Clio Award, 163

clown, 50, 71–72, *72*; Alda as, 95; unemployment related to, 87

Cohn, Sam, 172

Coke machine, 62, 63

college: "Abou Ben Adhem" at, 47; burlesque show in, 52–53; classes at, 46; contests at, 48; dialects in, 51–52; girlfriend in, 57–59; graduation from, 47, 65; invitation to, 44; Italian in, 50–51; jokes at, 45; Knotts in, 52–53; landlady at, 48; Lichello at, 47, 48–49; masochist menu in, 55–56; New York after, 47; "Oral Interpretation" in, 51; rabbits related to, 48; silent films at, 47; sketch actor in, 54–55; sleight of hand in, 53; "Speech" at, 46; theater at, 46, 57–58; TV in, 53–55; vaudeville in, 49;

About the Author

Paul Dooley is a veteran actor who, in his six-decade career, has appeared in movies, in television, and on the stage. He was a co-creator and head writer of *The Electric Company*, the award-winning TV show for the Children's Television Workshop. He is married to Winnie Holzman, who, with famed songwriter Stephen Schwartz, created the hit Broadway musical *Wicked*. More at www.pauldooleyactor.com